HOW TO STOP LIVING FOR THE APPLAUSE

How to Stop Living for the Applause

Holly G. Miller
and
Dennis E. Hensley

VINE
BOOKS

Servant Publications
Ann Arbor, Michigan

Vine Books is an imprint of Servant Publications especially
designed to serve Evangelical Christians.

Cover design by Michael Andaloro

Published by Servant Books
P.O. Box 8617
Ann Arbor, Michigan 48107

Printed in the United States of America
ISBN 0-89283-642-3
90 91 92 93 94   10 9 8 7 6 5 4 3 2 1

Library of Congress Cataloging-in-Publication Data

Miller, Holly.
  How to stop living for the applause / Holly G. Miller with
with Dennis E. Hensley.
      p.   cm.
    ISBN 0-89283-642-3
    1. Workaholism.   2. Women—Employment—
Psychological aspects.   3. Christian life—1960-
I. Hensley, Dennis E., 1948-   II. Title.
RC569.5.W67M54   1990
616.85′2—dc20   90-8490
                                                      CIP

Contents

Preface

THE FIRST LETTER CAME FROM a woman in South Carolina and simultaneously patted me on the back, chucked me on the chin, and wagged a finger under my nose. She liked my article on workaholism, wanted to assure me that mine was a controllable addiction, but warned me that it would be my "cross to bear" for the rest of my life. No wonder I liked the second letter better.

"Ouch!" it began. "Your story about workaholism sure hit home." She explained that she was the wage and benefits manager of a midsized hospital in the Midwest, and once each year she and her staff conducted round-the-clock employee meetings in order to explain changes in the group insurance package.

"I had arrived at work at 2:30 A.M. to talk with our third shifters and was running around like a maniac; not enough time, not enough time. . . . Someone had left your story on my desk, so I stole five minutes to glance at, then really read it. Wow! Did God ever speak to me through that article! I had known that at times my work was taking priority in my life, but the bluntness of your article made me realize that my family could *never* be replaced. I needed to change. Still, balance hasn't always been easy to obtain, you know?"

I knew.

Next came an invitation to speak to a Baptist women's group in Dallas. "We have a lot of members who share your, er, *fondness* for work," the caller said delicately. This was followed by a note from a man who demanded equal time.

Did I think that workaholism was just a woman's problem? he challenged. To change my mind, he gave me a piece of his.

Ironic. Twenty years after pastoral counselor Wayne Oates invented workaholism—the label, not the condition—the topic still nudges busy people to action. They defend, deny, and dismiss their addiction. And they do it with "Type A" gusto. Dr. Oates confessed his, er, *fondness* for work in a short article published in a 1968 issue of *Pastoral Psychology*. The response overwhelmed him, and a book resulted: *Confessions of a Workaholic*. It was geared to men. I shared my hidden addiction in a short article published in a 1988 issue of *Today's Christian Woman*. The barrage of mail amazed me, and a book has resulted: *How to Stop Living for the Applause*. It's geared to women.

To add a male perspective—since men work with us, live with us, and interact with us daily—I enlisted Dr. Dennis Hensley to help with the project. You'll notice we alternate writing chapters. Again, equal time. But Dennis is no newcomer to the topic of work. With twenty books and more than two thousand articles to his credit, he admits to having a, er, *fondness* for it. Among his books are *Positive Workaholism* (career motivation) and *How To Manage Your Time: Time Management Strategies for Active Christians*. He travels the country counseling and speaking on both.

Like most writers, Dennis and I deplore cliches. If we didn't, we might exhume something trite about yet another workaholism book ... something like, "here we go again" or "history repeats itself" or "back to square one." But our book is no rehash of Dr. Oates's book. Our purpose is not to say ditto to what was said two decades ago. Too much has happened since then. Women have changed, work has changed, and the way women view themselves and their work has also changed. In particular, Christian women have changed.

The only thing that hasn't changed is workaholism. It's still with us. And so are the rewards it provides and the guilt and stress it produces. But after two decades of examining the topic, new ways have been devised to harness workaholism, to integrate it into a balanced lifestyle, and to use it for positive results. These are the insights we want to share with you in this book.

ONE

The Hidden Addiction

*I've given up something in all these years. I don't play
very well. . . . I'm not a beach person. I know people who
just lie there and watch the ocean come in. I want to fix it
if it has a leak. I want to build something on the shore.*
—Erma Bombeck

NOBODY ASKED ME.

Those management experts who reported that Americans
waste five years of their lives waiting in lines, two years
trying to return phone calls, one year looking for lost articles,
and six months idling at traffic lights never knocked on the
Miller door or asked this lady of the house to fill out their
questionnaire. If they had, my answers might have skewed
their bell curve. At worst, I would have earned an end note at
the back of one of their chapters.

I never wait in lines because I know where the lines form
and I avoid them. You won't find me at the bank on Friday at
12:10 P.M. because I know local businesses distribute payroll
checks before lunch, and everyone heads for the driveups.
Everyone but me. I never grocery shop on Wednesday
because that's the day the coupons are published in the
newspaper, and bargain hunters want first dibs on the
specials.

Phone messages? They haven't been a problem since I programmed my answering machine to kick in after the second ring. Lost articles? It's a wonder I don't spend more time hunting for them, since as a writer I never throw away anything. Magazines, books, clippings, you name it; they're all in uneven stacks in our spare-bedroom-turned-home-office. But there's order in my chaos. Give me a minute to root around in my files and I generally can extract precisely what I'm looking for.

Six months at stoplights ... there I plead no contest. Traffic delays are out of my control, particularly since I live in Conrail country. But I've learned to make the best of the situation. Seldom do I get behind the wheel without first tossing in the back seat a non-fiction book to read or a wad of papers to grade. As I pull out of the driveway I pop a learning tape into the cassette deck and hope I'll be motivated, enlightened, or inspired by the time I reach my destination. Currently I'm working my way through Dr. Ken Cooper's series on fitness. He's making me feel guilty about my diet which is light on fiber and heavy on anything that can be fixed in a crockpot.

I've always viewed time as an awesome gift from God— priceless, because it can't be bought; elusive, because it slips away; and frustrating, because it can never be lured back, in spite of my promises to use it better if only given a second chance. I've decided that in some ways time is like money, and in other ways it couldn't be more different. It can be spent, invested, squandered, and lost. It can be appreciated but it can never appreciate; it can be divided but never multiplied, it can be saved but never banked.

In the writing classes I teach at Anderson University, my students have learned not to play with time. They're assured some red ink if they wax creative about *long* years, *short* days, or *brief* minutes.

"A year has 365 days, a day has twenty-four hours, and a minute has sixty seconds," I admonish them. "Nothing you can do will ever change that. Only your perception of time can change. Depending on how you use your time, a year can *seem* to drag, a day can *seem* to fly, and a minute can *seem* to evaporate."

In the Old Testament the psalmist writes, "Remember how short you have made man's lifespan" (Psalm 89:47, *The Living Bible*). If only I could forget. A study by a Washington, D.C., research team claims the average American woman can expect a lifespan of seventy-nine years, which translates to seven years longer than the average American man and thirty years longer than the typical woman in Bangladesh. In spite of our edge, I panic at the numbers. They remind me that I've worked through half my allotment of time without accomplishing half my aspirations of success. Breathlessly I look for ways to prune more waste and pour more meaning into my minutes.

I'm a recovering workaholic. I say "recovering" because workaholism can be controlled but never cured. I say "workaholic" because I take my obligations—work, marriage, family, church—seriously. Sometimes *too* seriously. I often assume too many duties, then fret when I feel fragmented. "If you're going to do something, do it right," is one of my favorite pieces of advice. But when I apply it to myself, "doing it right" usually means pushing for perfection. I never quite make it, but I keep trying.

I'm a high achiever who knows that high-achievement, perfectionism, and workaholism aren't identical, but they're very much related. One can lead to another and each can become an addiction. Unlike a lot of addictions, high-achievement, perfectionism, and workaholism are accepted in all the right circles. They usually earn generous strokes and occasional "atta-girls" from people who matter. For me, these people include my editors who expect me to meet deadlines; my students who claim me as a role model as they juggle jobs, classes, and campus activities; my family who likes to eat on time and in an orderly kitchen; and various leaders of service organizations who recruit me for their boards, committees, and task forces. (Like most workaholics, I seldom say no to a good cause.)

I get mixed signals on workaholism. Positive reinforcement for the "addiction" is everywhere. While some companies offer treatment and counseling to substance abusers, they offer bonuses and plaques to work addicts. While the recovering alcohol or drug abuser can go "cold turkey" and abstain from his substance, the recovering work addict can't kick his habit and abstain from his job. He can only hope to curb, not kill, his insatiable appetite for whatever it is that he does from 9 to 5, 8 to 6, 7 to 7, or worse. Instead of being enrolled in a support group that will shore up his efforts to shed his dependency, he and his dependency are used as examples for peers to follow.

Christians have struggled with the problem of overwork for centuries. In fact, we're still not convinced it *is* a problem. We tend to think too much of a good thing can be an even better thing. Especially if it's related to service, family, or our profession. We trade cliches with friends and urge them to keep their "nose to the grindstone" because "there's no such thing as a free lunch." We prompt our children to "remember the Protestant work ethic," and we tell them cute stories about the fiesty engine that could, and the little red hen that worked hard and was rewarded well for it. We quote them proverbs about the tireless little ant who still serves as a role model for us. On Sunday morning we sing wonderful old hymns that prod us to "Come, labor on" and "Work, for the night is coming."

Workaholism is so common that it has launched at least one spin-off industry. Products that support a breathless workstyle glut the marketplace. My favorite workaholic "tool" comes from a Denver company. It is a carseat that prevents a portable computer from sliding around in an automobile. This ingenious gizmo enables the workaholic to be productive as he or she frets away those six months at traffic lights. While some of us merely read books or listen to Dr. Cooper scold us about our lack of fiber, the high-tech job junkie can tap away at spreadsheets as he waits for the red light to change or the freight train to pass. Now, *that's* time management. Embellishments are available, of course. Mini fax machines and downsized copiers can be attached to a car's cellular phone to round out the mobile workspace.

Even more innovation is in our future if we're to believe the Campbell Soup Company and its forecast that in another decade about 25 percent of automobiles will be equipped with microwave ovens. Already perfected is a power converter that allows a commuter or carpooler to save time by plugging in her hair dryer or curling iron and grooming herself enroute.

Just as workaholism has prompted a unique support industry, that same support industry has generated a second tier of products. Companies now manufacture workaholic toys, not tools, to help people look as if they're work-crazed executives even if they aren't. Bogus beepers are one example; another is the Cellular Phoney, the brainchild of a bright California entrepreneur who came up with a car phone lookalike that costs less than the real thing because it isn't. At last report, more than 45,000 people had bought the fake phone and antenna set and could be seen speeding down highways talking to themselves.

There is even an answering machine for your car phone. When you call it, a recording comes on and says, "I'm sorry I cannot take your call right now, but I'm at home. As soon as I leave home, I'll return your call."

All of this craziness seems to underscore the idea that workaholism is good, something to aspire to, and that the next best thing to being one is looking like one. Such a mindset has been with us for years and shows no sign of easing. When Dr. Marilyn Machlowitz announced plans to write a book analyzing workaholics more than a decade ago, an aggressive young professional enthusiastically asked if the book would show him how to become one. Since then, dozens of books and articles have been written on the subject. Most have self-help themes and are written by men who assume that workaholism is a serious condition that is seriously suffered only by men. Don't believe it. Workaholism among women has merely been hidden because women have been less visible, and their accomplishments haven't always been marked by promotions or tracked on the business pages of the local newspaper. But all that is changing.

Workaholism doesn't suddenly appear when a woman jumps into the job market. My husband still teases me about my early workaholic tendencies that surfaced when we were newlyweds. Determined to transform our sparsely furnished duplex into a decorator's showplace, I entered what we now call my Ceramic Period. I wasn't satisfied until I had created a fruit stack, bust of Cicero, or ashtray (no one smoked) for every table. When I ran out of space, I began stashing away pottery dust catchers as Christmas gifts for all my new relatives. By November, our apartment looked like a cross between the storage vault of an archeological dig and a trading post on an Indian reservation.

A passion for canning replaced ceramics. I sealed row after row of corn relish. The problem was, no one in my family even *liked* corn relish, which was just as well because I couldn't bear to have a vacant spot interrupt my perfectly arranged pantry shelves. I told myself that the next time we were invited to a pitch-in, I was ready.

Workaholics always live in the future. We love to plan and prepare, but we don't know how to relax and enjoy. We're like Martha, who welcomed Jesus and his disciples into her home and then spent most of the time fretting over dinner. Rather than sitting at Jesus' feet to hear his teaching, Martha chose to work. She expected to be praised for her efforts, but instead, Jesus gently pointed out that she was too concerned with details, and that her sister Mary had made the wiser decision when she had chosen to sit and listen. "There is really only one thing worth being concerned about," said Jesus. "Mary has discovered it" (Luke 10:42, *The Living Bible*).

I didn't discover it for years. Too often I'd let my husband take our children to Sunday school so I could have two hours of uninterrupted time to run the sweeper, wax the floor, or iron everyone's clothes for the next day.

The pace was stepped up considerably when I reentered the workforce after our two boys began school. My field was journalism, a profession characterized by constant deadlines. While some writers view deadlines as burdens, I saw them as blessings. I loved the pressure. The challenge of setting and meeting goals became a game, and I was disappointed when I won because that meant the rules were suspended. Rather than being relieved at the conclusion of a project, I was at loose ends until I had replaced it with a new one. I found that when I had less to worry about, I worried about less more. I had to keep busy. Sometimes I purposely missed a deadline in order to hold onto the tension until another writing assignment came along to take its place.

Skeptics sometimes ask me to elaborate on the seriousness of my workaholism. I tell them this: I used to dread vacations, and I'd regularly volunteer to staff the newspaper office on Christmas and New Year's Day ("*Somebody* has to do it," I'd insist). I used to place reading material in key places around the house so I could read as I put on my makeup, opened cans, ate breakfast, and brushed my teeth. I never did one job at a time. Typically, I'd polish my fingernails while grading papers as my husband and I watched the six o'clock news after dinner. At one point in my life I was working as editor of our city's newspaper, attending graduate school, moonlighting as a free-lance magazine writer, teaching a continuing education course in creative writing, overseeing our twelve-room house, and trying (but not always succeeding) to be a good companion to my husband and two sons.

"How do you do it?" people often asked with admiration.

"I wish I were as organized as you are," friends would moan.

"You're a regular supermom," was a familiar compliment.

"Your family must be so proud of you," was my favorite.

Actually, my family was surprisingly silent on the subject. All three of the "men" in my life seemed less and less impressed when I would announce, bleary-eyed at the breakfast table, that I had stayed up until 3 A.M. to complete an article. Their enthusiasm didn't nearly match mine when I would finish writing one book and promptly would be offered a contract for a sequel.

"Aren't you proud of me?" I remember prodding them one Saturday when my ego hadn't received its quota of strokes.

"Sure, Mom," was the dutiful response from the boys.

I was underwhelmed.

"That was a lukewarm answer if I've ever heard one," I complained.

No comment.

"Name one time when my work schedule has caused a problem," I challenged. Three pairs of eyes met in consultation. *Should we* or *shouldn't we?* they seemed to ask.

"Well, Honey, there was our second honeymoon to Hawaii," my husband Phil began tentatively. "You practically worked double time for a month before we took off because you said you wanted to leave with a clear conscience and a clean desk. Then you spent every day on the beach scribbling in your notebook so you'd be ahead when we got home."

Ouch.

I knew I could count on Charlie, our older son, for a kind word. After all, he already had announced his intention to attend Indiana University as I had done years earlier, and major in journalism just like Mom. Friends jokingly called him my clone.

"I remember when our band won the state marching

contest and you weren't there because you were in New York City interviewing somebody," he offered.

So much for clones.

I turned to Whitney, my short, dark, and handsome one. As our younger son, he had escaped the ceramic and corn-relish periods but had borne the brunt of my newspaper years. I held up my hand to be spared memories of missed Little League games and school birthday parties when my husband brought the cupcakes and Hawaiian punch. Neither did he need to remind me of my car pool obligations that too often were juggled, traded, or fulfilled by friends because my schedule had me in three places at once.

Stung by my family's reaction, I realized that each family member had suffered from my work compulsion. I started to argue my case. How could they even suggest that I had fallen short of anyone's expectations? I retaliated in my usual way: I vowed to work harder than ever to prove them wrong. I'd show them... just watch. It was as if I were calling their bluff. "How can I be a failure? Look at my accomplishments. See what I've done. Listen to the applause."

But the wrong people were applauding, and I knew it.

My second impulse was to drop out. In typical all-or-nothing fashion, I decided to refuse future writing assignments, cancel the class I was scheduled to teach, and send my regrets regarding speaking engagements. I had no business sharing the "secrets of my success" with anyone anyway. Just as I had compulsively thrown myself into my work, I now was determined to attack retirement with equal passion.

Fortunately, good sense and a good friend stopped me. Georgia is a Christian counselor who had once taken my creative writing class for her personal enrichment. That in itself had impressed me. How could a successful wife, mother, and businesswoman find time to attend an enrichment class at night?

"For balance," she had told me at the conclusion of our

first session. Remembering that response, I called her after my family confrontation.

"I helped you once with balance," I reminded her. "Can you return the favor?" She agreed.

The first hurdle I had to overcome was recognizing workaholism for what it is. I had to strip it of its mystique, reduce it to a weakness, and then deal with it. This was no small task.

Three years after facing my addiction, I'm still struggling with it. I'm improving, but I know that no quick fix exists. At Georgia's suggestion I've cleared some clutter from my calendar, established priorities among my activities, and half-jokingly written "Stop to smell the roses" on several lines of my daily planner. I've learned when to say yes and when to say no. If in doubt, I remember Georgia's comparison of a woman to a violin. When no stress is placed on a violin's strings, the sound is dull and flat. When too much tension is applied, the "music" is shrill and strident. But when the right amount of pressure is exerted, the melody is beautiful and balanced.

I still hit a sour note or two. Occasionally I lose my place, improvise, and have to stop and review the score. When I do, I generally find I'm not in tune with what I've set as my new goals. The harmony is suspended until I slow the tempo. Like any good musician-in-training, I improve with experience. But most importantly, I now understand the value of practicing every day. I may not be a maestro yet, but through this book I'm ready to share what I've learned so far from some very good teachers.

TWO

Double Standard: If You're Okay, Why Aren't I Okay?

Why can't a woman (ta dum, ta dum)
be more like a man? (ta dum, ta dum)
—Professor Henry Higgins

I RECOGNIZED HER HARUMPH INSTANTLY.

"Have a seat," I said, even before looking up and over my glasses. She moved from the doorway into my office and stiffly lowered herself into the visitor's chair. We had met on Monday, the first day of the semester, and two classes later we were about to have our first (of many) confrontations. Our teacher-student record got off to a scratchy start when she angrily thrust a fistful of papers at me. I took a quick look.

"Your assignment," I acknowledged.

"My *'B,'* " she retorted. Then she leaned forward and with an icy glare informed me, "Professor Miller, I don't *get* B's, thank you, I have *never* gotten B's, and I have no intention of starting now, especially with some silly little newswriting class."

Hmmm. I wasn't sure if I had just been issued a threat, a warning, or a challenge. Whatever it was, I was certain this visit was no welcome-to-campus gesture extended by her, an upperclassman, to me, a newly arrived professor of communications.

Just as she let me know on that cloudy Friday afternoon in January 1986 that she planned to maintain her straight *A* average with or without my cooperation, I silently vowed that we would emerge as friends from my "silly little newswriting class." Five months later we had both accomplished our goals. She graduated *summa cum laude* with a *B*-free academic record, and I attended the commencement dinner hosted by her parents for her closest pals. In between, we had shoehorned many long discussions. Sometimes the topic was newswriting, but more often it was our shared affliction—work addiction.

After graduation Judie completed a master's degree with honors and accepted a management position with a large utility firm in Chicago. We still keep in touch. Whenever she's tempted to verbally bash her boss, she counts to ten and calls me on the phone instead. We talk a lot.

"What drives you?" I asked her once during a leisurely heart-to-heart, courtesy of her WATS line. She had just updated me on a horrendous week that had included working through lunch, lugging a document-laden briefcase aboard the commuter train at night, and taking a beeper home as her weekend companion. The latter allowed her to be "on call" until Monday morning when the grind would begin again.

"I've always been this way; I've always pushed hard," was her answer. She explained that her voracious appetite for work dated back to preschool days when a pediatrician diagnosed her as "bright," and recommended to her parents that she should start school at age four. It wasn't long after enrollment that she learned her many talents didn't include sports. Today she credits part of her drive to the lack of coordination that became painfully evident on the kinder-garten playground. When she figured out, back in the late 1960s, that she would never turn a perfect cartwheel or send a softball airborne over a distant fence, she directed her considerable energy to another area. Not satisfied merely to be "pretty good" at anything, she looked for a niche where she could excel. Books seemed to be the answer. She set about to consume the Elgin, Illinois, public library.

"I was the kid who always raised her hand in class. I had all the answers. The teacher would say, 'I know *you* know, Judie, but let's see if anybody else does.' I remember thinking at the start of each school year, *Just wait till you get to know me.* It would take a teacher about a week, then I'd be her pet."

Judie is an only child (psychologists believe that oldest and only children are most vulnerable to workaholism and perfectionism), and her parents let her know very early what was expected of her. Simply put: Everything. An excellent violinist, she also is a gifted vocalist, a confident public speaker, a knowledgeable Bible student, a computer whiz . . . and the list goes on. She claims her mother as her role model and herself as her mom's "main project."

"In her job, my mother has always been the secretary in the office who knows everything that goes on, can send you exactly to the right place, and can organize absolutely anything," says Judie. "She used to sit down with me when I was little and watch me do my homework. She'd check the results and show me how to apply myself. Her work habits became my work habits. And they're still in place after all these years. For instance, I can't function at a messy desk. I have to have everything in files and every file has to be in its alphabetical place. I can only work on one thing at a time and when that's done, I move on to the next project."

Although Judie is not a psychologist, she is exactly on target in crediting her mother as the molding force in her life. Andree Aelion Brooks in *Children of Fast-Track Parents* (Viking,

1989) points out that some parents equate their children's success to their own success and, to that end, "the child replaces business ventures as a goal" (p. 211). She quotes psychologist Bettie Youngs, who explains, "The child becomes the achievement—the job, the career, the status symbol." These parents are most happy when their children emulate them in action, thought, and deed. In Judie's case, her mother was scrupulous about personal organization, and to win her mother's approval, Judie became equally scrupulous.

"Lists! I'd go crazy if I didn't make a list every Friday of what I plan to accomplish the following week," admits Judie. "My mind would be flooded by obligations, and I'd wonder, 'When am I going to do this? How am I going to get this done?' Making a list is a lot like clearing space on a computer hard disk by storing things on a floppy disk. You free up memory that way; it's written down, so you don't have to worry about it."

Judie's parents—I've been in their company several times—are wonderful people. While it might be easy to label her mother and father as overbearing or to depict them as insensitive, selfish, or aggressive, such descriptive words don't fit. They adore Judie, and when it comes to their "main project" they simply have never been able to remain passively on the sidelines. Instead, they resemble an intense little cheering block of two, always poised on the fifty-yard line, clapping enthusiastically, and calling the plays as the action unfolds. The problem has been that Mom often has urged Judie to go one way, while Dad has coached her in another direction. Judie, trying to please both, has worn herself out running back and forth between "goal" posts. The goals usually weren't hers, but were Mom's and Dad's instead.

In college, she majored in business for Dad (she would have preferred English) and continued her music studies for Mom. She was expected to assert herself in class and to compete aggressively for top honors in tough accounting, statistics, and computer science courses. At odds with all this professional moxie was her image. She was always dressed in ultra-feminine clothes—high heels, bright-colored sundresses in the summer, frilly blouses and slim skirts in the fall. Her hair was long and curly and framed her pretty face and ever-dazzling smile. All this for Mom.

On the surface, Judie seemed remarkably composed. How well I remember bumping into her on campus during final exam week of her senior year. Other students looked frazzled; girls forgot about makeup, boys neglected to shave. All were bleary-eyed from exhausting marathons with unfinished term papers and unread textbooks.

But not Judie. Her hair was perfectly groomed, her makeup was impeccably applied, her smile was confidently in place. "What, me worry?" seemed to be her line. Just as she worked doubletime to be all things to her parents, so did she labor to please her professors. She always kept up with her reading, completed her assignments, and turned in her papers on time. So final exam week was just another opportunity for her to shine. And shine she did.

I never would have guessed that within a few weeks of her jubilant commencement party, Judie would come dangerously close to losing control of her life. But more about her great awakening later.

GREAT EXPECTATIONS

In the ever-popular Lerner and Lowe musical, "My Fair Lady," a bewildered Professor Henry Higgins cavorts around the stage half talking, half singing the question, "Why can't a woman be more like a man?" I've often thought that 'enry 'iggins might have found his answer much quicker if only he had asked Virginia Chapman instead of Colonel Pickering.

Like Professor Higgins, Professor Chapman is a speech communications expert. I've learned a lot from Ginny, and one of the most valuable lessons has been that sometimes "speech" is silent and involves much more than the rain in Spain. Ginny teaches students at two universities not only to read body language but also to decipher the silent visual messages that bombard all of us in advertisements. She's particularly interested in how women are depicted by the media. She believes that some advertisements pressure women in the same way that Judie's parents unwittingly pressured their only daughter. The media's message is this: *"You must be all things to all people, and you must strive to do all things well."* Women such as Judie who hear a similar refrain at home are especially vulnerable to the media's message. To them, the media are underscoring and adding impetus to an all-too-familiar directive. The advice is the same: *"Push, push, push for perfection."* The messages they receive in person and in print are in harmony. One reinforces and amplifies the other.

To ignite a lively class discussion, Ginny sometimes tosses out this question: "Are the media like mirrors, accurately reflecting images of who we are and what we look like? Or are we reflections of the media, taking our cues from ads, articles, and television shows and striving to become what the media tell us we're supposed to be?"

Ginny doesn't claim to know the answer, but just for fun she collects old magazines to illustrate how a woman's place, as seen in advertisements, has changed over the years. As to who initiated the change—the women depicted or the Madison Avenue gurus who do the depicting—it's debatable, but the contrast between women of a few decades ago and women of today is fascinating. So, too, are the similarities. No wonder some of us feel driven.

Which only raises more questions: Who's in the driver's seat? Are women choosing their own destinations and mapping their own strategy as to how to get where they want to go? Or are they passively being taken for a ride? Are they, like Judie, allowing someone else to choose their directions and set their goals for them?

Ginny's interest in ads from the past is catching. Sometimes when my role as a contributing editor to *The Saturday Evening Post* takes me to company headquarters in Indianapolis, I spend my lunch hour in the archives with a sandwich, an apple, and dusty volumes of past *Posts* and the magazine's formidable competitors.

Look over my shoulder and see what I've found.

Life magazine, March 14, 1960. An advertisement for Kem-Tone wall paint is like a short drama that unfolds via pictures with members of a model family as its "stars." The cast: Mom, Dad, and a pre-school daughter. It's morning and Mom is kissing Dad goodbye as he leaves for the office. She's already dressed for a full day of chores in her high heels, shirtwaist, and apron. But today's housework includes a surprise. Small pictures, inserted in the ad, show her smiling as she begins rolling yellow paint on dingy gray walls.

By the time Dad returns that evening, *voila!* the room is a vision of saffron. Mom, the proud painter, is pointing to herself. Dad is simultaneously holding one of her hands and looking incredulously at the walls. The silent message comes from Dad: "Is it possible that my wife has done all this? She's found time to do her usual housewifey tasks, plus paint the house, and still look gorgeous for me?" Daughter is dutifully holding Dad's soft hat and looking incredulously at Mom. Her silent message seems to be a proud, "That's my mom! Whatta role model. When I grow up I'm going to be just like her." The reader can almost smell pot roast and all the fixin's in the kitchen. Is there nothing this gal can't do?

Saturday Evening Post, November 23, 1963. Mom may wear a lot of hats signifying a lot of duties, but she still has only one pair of hands to perform those duties. What does she need to help her become even *more* effective than she already is? A new line of kitchen appliances, of course. At the top of the page are four pictures showing Mom's various roles. In the first picture she's holding a baby and has two stairstep toddlers attached to her legs; in the second photo, she's dressed in her best chemise and is being bussed on the cheek by her tuxedo-clad hubby; third, she has a mixing bowl in one hand and a gourmet cookbook in the other; finally, she's donned a hostess gown (I'll bet she made it) and is offering crackers and a cheeseball to company. If you don't get the message, the words help. "You can be an even *better* mother, wife, cook, and hostess with these three Kelvinators." Pictures of a fridge, stove, and dishwasher let you know which three tools will help make the little woman ubiquitous.

Was Mom perfect back in the 1960s and did the ads reflect that perfection? Or were the ads showing us what a perfect woman—1960s style—*should* look like, in the hope that we women would use the ads as a yardstick by which to measure ourselves? Both the 1960 and the 1963 ads send a common, silent message: A woman is a source of particular delight when she stretches and expands to fill new roles as well as meet the old ones with ease and expertise.

She's a wife, lover, mother, cook, seamstress, nurse, cheerleader, housekeeper, hostess, even painter of saffron walls.

She always wears a smile, and generally an apron; she's never content to be merely wonderful, she's always working to be even better at what she already does very well.

Being good enough isn't good enough for her.

She aims to please and she always hits her mark.

Time warp: Twenty-five years later, 1989. A television commercial for United Airlines begins with Mom guiding her daughter to the day-care center. Her apron has been replaced by pinstripes and a floppy bow tie. The cheeseball is gone; in its place a briefcase. She kisses her daughter goodbye and makes sure the little girl's homemade lunch is safely clutched in little fingers, then she rushes to the airport, boards a United jet, and is next seen wowing a roomful of male execs with a dynamite presentation. She moves deftly from podium to flip chart with no one but us noticing that she consults her watch from time to time. Right on cue she exits the meeting, dashes to the airport to catch the jet that allows her to arrive unruffled at the day-care center as the last activity of the afternoon concludes. The daughter slips her little hand into Mom's and looks up adoringly. Silent message: "Whatta role model."

MEET MS. MOM

If we're to believe the media, Mom hasn't traded duties as she's moved from the sixties to the nineties, she's merely added to them. The media correctly reflect the trend toward working moms (10.5 million preschoolers have mothers who are employed, and that number is expected to grow to 15 million by 1995), but Mom has kept the old job description and merely annexed the new. The media may show her following in the footsteps of men, but she's walking doubletime to keep up and she's doing it all in spike heels. Like Judie, she's dashing from one set of goals to another and trying to score in all fields of activity.

But let's not be too hard on secular advertisers. Christian media are just as guilty as their worldly counterparts— advertising or otherwise—in nudging female readers toward a non-stop work ethic. I'm reminded of a prominent Christian women's magazine that was preparing an article about a successful businesswoman and her assorted accomplishments. It was a typical "superwoman" profile in the Kem-Tone/Kelvinator tradition. It touted the woman's success as a wife, mother of two children, and owner of a Washington-based consulting firm. In the course of the interview the woman mentioned that she employed a live-in nanny to care for her children and to cook for the family.

Since the woman being interviewed had a job that often took her on the road, the presence of full-time help provided efficiency in the kitchen and continuity in the nursery. But after much discussion, the magazine's editor decided to delete all reference to the housekeeper because it detracted from the "typicalness" of the woman. Mom didn't seem quite so super when it was known that she depended on outside help. And, reasoned the managing editor, there was the risk that readers might not approve of a Christian mother delegating family duties to others. After all, the Bible says, *"She* looks well to the ways of *her* household" (Proverbs 31:27), not she "hireth" someone to do it. So the information was omitted and the myth was perpetuated.

The image of the little lady who painted dingy walls yellow, jetted to business meetings between carpool runs, and made clothes for herself and cheeseballs for company remained intact. Only now she owned a consulting firm in Washington. Anyone who read the published article about the talented businesswoman surely would feel sufficiently impressed, in awe, and *inadequate.*

I've been guilty of contributing to the myth myself. In the twenty years that I've written articles for daily newspapers, national magazines, and corporate publications, my speciality has been profiles of successful women. I've sought out these women, played up their victories, ticked off their honors, and sidestepped their defeats. I've interviewed Barbara Mandrell ("She's a gourmet cook, she's the mother of three, she organizes charity softball games, and she performs two hundred concerts a year!"); Sandi Patti ("She sings, she writes music, she's building a children's clinic in her hometown, she even has *twins!*"); Debby Boone ("She's the daughter/wife/mom who lights up the record charts and now writes best-selling children's books!''); and Marabel Morgan ("She's the toast of the talk-show circuit, the wife, mom, and marriage counselor who talked us into go-go boots, baby-doll pajamas, and buying *The Total Woman!*'').

The problem with all this hype is that it undergirds the belief that a woman must be extraordinary in *everything* if she is to be noteworthy in anything. Whereas readers who are *not* perfectionists might skim such an article about Barbara Mandrell and decide that she's a likable and talented entertainer, perfectionists see much more. They see vindication for their own breathless pace as they link the performer's success with her willingness to work night and day. They extract and amplify the paragraphs about Barbara's determination as a child to learn to play every instrument in her dad's music store, her insistence on booking a concert when she was still limping from her serious auto accident, and her plans simultaneously to write a book, make a movie, and launch another tour. They dwell on her remark that she's not *really* satisfied with a performance until she is properly drenched with sweat.

In my years as editor of a General Motors magazine I constantly wrote and published articles about female employees who were holding their own as engineers, earning their stripes as supervisors, and making their ways as sales reps while enthusiastically and expertly overseeing home and family. The more successful they were, the better candidates they were for my articles . . . especially if they were making inroads into areas previously perceived to be for men only. The occasional dark side to these upbeat stories—divorce, burnout, stress—was omitted from the formula. It didn't "fit." After all, these were motivational articles designed to stroke deserving employees and to inspire the rank and file to follow suit. In retrospect, I wonder if they also didn't have a negative effect on over-achievers who took the articles at face value and used them as blueprints for success. I wonder, too, if these same stories didn't frustrate women at the other extreme—the undereducated single parents who were locked into assembly-line jobs by a lack of time and a shortage of training.

The same distorted picture that is portrayed in magazine articles and in advertisements is a mainstay of network television series. Not only are women depicted as high-achievers who successfully shoulder a mixed bag of duties, but their bigger-than-life efforts also bring greater-than-normal rewards. Key characters in popular sitcoms and dramas often are no more than updated versions of the Kem-Tone/Kelvinator heroine who by now have moved out of the home and into high-powered professions.

For instance, Angela Lansbury's character in "Murder, She Wrote" cooks, cleans, gardens, and does community service as many traditional women do, but she also solves sticky murder cases and writes best-selling mysteries in her off-hours. Jill Eikenberry's role in "L.A. Law" has her playing a confident, aggressive attorney who is intelligent, attractive, sexy, happily married, and a loving mother. (I've interviewed Jill and she admits to following a strong work ethic but nothing like that of her cooly assertive character, Ann Kelsey.)

Such high achievers hardly reflect the "typical" woman in America, although many women who have workaholic or perfectionistic tendencies may use these bloated caricatures as yardsticks and find themselves sadly lacking by comparison. According to *American Demographics* magazine (June 1989, pp. 25-27), if there is such a thing as an average American woman she certainly isn't a famous sleuth and she doesn't look like Jill Eikenberry. Neither does she organize charity softball games, underwrite children's clinics, or light up the pop music charts. She isn't particularly beautiful (in fact, she has brown hair, wears glasses, weighs 143 pounds, and is on a diet), isn't rich (she makes less than $20,000 a year), hasn't achieved entrepreneurial success (hers is a sales, administrative, or technical job), and she doesn't enjoy all the trappings of a glamorous life (she drives an eight-year-old car, lives in a twenty-five-year-old home, and faces three and a half hours of household chores and child care every day after work).

AND THEN THERE'S MR. MOM

How have men fared at the hands of the media? While women are shown in a serious light as they assume men's roles, men are shown in a comic light when the situation is reversed. They're all thumbs as they attempt to cook, change a diaper, or run a sweeper. A woman who fails in a business setting would hardly be material for comedy writers, but put a guy in a kitchen, add eggs, and you've whipped up some heavy mirth. Anyone who doubts this hasn't seen such films as "Mr. Mom," "Three Men and a Baby" and "Kramer vs. Kramer." The gags are old, but the audience still laughs, probably in sympathy. Men aren't supposed to succeed at "women's work," after all.

Men can watch movies or TV shows about how clumsy the brotherhood is at cooking, house cleaning, and child care and they can laugh out loud at the situations. They are not threatened by them. Their attitude is, "I wouldn't want to be known as an 'expert' at changing diapers, anyway." Rather than demeaning the man who stumbles through a woman's workday, the "humorous" situation *demeans the work instead.* Because of this, many women have also come to think of child-rearing, homemaking, and cooking as jobs without power or prestige. They want to do what men do. And to fail would be to fail at gaining prestige.

Times have changed, and television and the press can take credit for breaking down some barriers. However, they also must take the heat for creating some false images. The truth is, *all* women cannot *always* do what men do. To portray it otherwise is unrealistic and unfair to women who feel they need to emulate TV and film role models as much as their mothers once felt the pressure to pattern themselves after June Cleaver and Harriet Nelson. Hear what people in the field have to say:

Terry Bain, a Michigan State Police officer, notes, "Women continually challenged the law enforcement system until they were granted the right to become squad car patrol officers. That's a shame. When a 109-pound female officer is sent into a bar to subdue and arrest a 240-pound drunken steelworker, she usually gets her face smashed in. I fail to see what she has proven by that."

Todd Boswell, owner of a factory in Indiana, recalls, "I was harassed month after month by women's groups about the fact that I wasn't hiring women to do any of the heavy construction projects in our main plant. They kept saying that women were as rugged and hardy as men. I didn't believe it, but finally I gave in and hired three women. The women worked hard but the jobs nearly killed them. The crazy thing about it, however, was that after I had hired these three 'equally rugged' women, I was told I would need to install extra lights in my company parking lot and hire a night watchman so that these women could get to their cars safely after the midnight shift. Now if that isn't a contradiction of terms, I don't know what is."

My point is not to berate men or women. I've always believed that James Beard could equal any woman in a kitchen, that James Dobson knew as much about raising children as any mom, and that Bob Avilla could clean and fix up homes as well as any full-time homemaker. I also believe that Connie Chung can report national news as accurately as any male reporter, that Steffi Graf is as intelligent a tennis player as any man on the court, and that Sandra Day O'Connor is as astute a Supreme Court justice as her eight masculine colleagues. My objective, like Ginny Chapman, is to have us analyze the media with a critical eye and ask,

"Who indeed, is shaping the viewpoints?" Are the messages that are being sent electronically and via print media honest communications? Or, are these messages creating unreasonable expectations, and are they heaping too heavy a burden on women who already demand too much of themselves?

One more point before we let the media off the hook: At the same time that they have provided women with role models who are difficult—even impossible—to equal, they've deprived women of one of the most important options available.

"What we've done is gotten rid of the role models for girls who want to be homemakers," says Chapman. "I know a woman who has never held a job outside her home since she was married. She has three children, does laundry every day, runs errands, and cooks. She's defensive about what she does. She says she works hard and no one respects what she accomplishes. I think that's unfortunately true. If you ask your children's friends to tell you what their mothers do, they feel pressured to respond with something other than 'homemaker.' In advertisements and on television everybody has a job. Look at the Cosby family—the 'model family'—and the mother is a lawyer. What happened to 'Leave It to Beaver' moms?"

DISREGARD THIS MESSAGE

Other kinds of messages, beyond those created by the media, also push and prod women to set incredibly high standards for themselves. According to Dr. Shad Helmstetter, author of *What to Say When You Talk to Your Self*, "In a recent year it was estimated that more than $200 million worth of self-help books and materials were purchased in the U.S. alone." These included videotapes with energy-charged titles such as "How to Be a Winner" and "The Do's and Don'ts of Top Achievers"; audiotapes that tell listeners how "Nice Guys Finish Rich" and "How to Get What You Want"; books such as *Believe and Achieve, Leadership Secrets of Attila the Hun, Office Warfare,* and *The Achievement Challenge: How to Be a 10 in Business. Success* magazine offers articles that motivate readers to "Grab Your Share," "Seize the Moment," and "Market Yourself; You Are the Product."

Some of these messages aren't intended for high-achievers, but are aimed at persons who need to boost their productivity. However, it's the over-achievers who seize the advice and claim it as their own. Often the buyers of these motivational books, tapes, and leadership seminars are work-prone job junkies who are already motivated and productive. Rather than igniting a spark in low-achievers, such products and programs merely fan the flames already burning out of control in over-achievers.

"The workaholic woman may listen to the motivational speaker and not realize that she's already doing what the speaker suggests," says Ginny Chapman. "She takes it to heart and thinks she has to do more. She doesn't sort out the message and understand that she's not the audience for the advice. She may have already reached her limit."

Occasionally the workaholic Christian woman totally misinterprets or twists a message and sees support for her work ethic even when it isn't there. She reads Proverbs 31 and decides that she must match, as closely as possible, the description of the "virtuous wife." Anything short of total accomplishment is total failure. The rewards sound wonderful—the praise of her husband, the blessings of her children, the respect of her neighbors—but in reality her efforts may bring her only frustration and burnout. Rare is the women who can succeed in being a perfect helpmate for her spouse, a flawless home manager, a talented supervisor of people, a shrewd businesswoman, a dedicated social servant, a wise counselor, and an energetic mother. Yet some keep trying. The tasks may change with time—spinner of flax and planter of a vineyard in biblical days, painter of yellow walls or L.A. lawyer in contemporary times—but the incredibly heavy burden remains the same.

"It's like space travel," says Ginny Chapman. "We only can go so fast before the vehicle comes apart. The work-aholic suffers physical and mental anguish when she realizes that she can't do any more than she's already doing."

TAKING CONTROL

Usually the rationalization that she's met her limit doesn't come easily for the perfectionist. For my young friend, Judie, awareness began a few weeks after her triumphant *summa cum laude* graduation from college. In her own words:

"It happened the hard way. The summer before my first year of graduate school I was juggling seven different part-time jobs and obligations. I'd start at 6:30 in the morning, work until noon at one job, eat my lunch in the car enroute to another job, squeeze in a summer school class in the afternoon, and go home at night to work on several free-lance projects. I had no time for friends, no time for fun, no time for me.

"When I started grad school that September with a full load of classes, I was having trouble with my concentration. It became as hard for me to pray or read the Bible or do a Bible study as it was to research a term paper. I couldn't produce anything. I'd work four or five hours on a two-page paper that I used to be able to do in an hour. Even then it wasn't any good, and that was frustrating. About March I had reached the point where I was downright scared. I had no energy. It was as if my body were saying, 'Sorry, but I can't do this anymore.' For the first time in my life I wanted to throw up my hands, quit, and go home to Mom and Dad with the news that I had failed."

Instead, she made a decision to change.

"It wasn't my first choice . . . my first choice would have been to keep on being superwoman. But I realized that wasn't going to work anymore," she says. "I restructured my life and set some new priorities. I became more sensitive to my internal alarm system that warned me when I had become too engrossed in my work. I learned to read the signs. Now when I sense myself becoming fragmented, I pull back. That's when I go home at night, kick off my shoes, watch television, and go to bed early."

Whereas most college grad students feel successful when they pull an *A* in a tough class, Judie knew she had succeeded when she received her first *B* and suffered no trauma from it. The world didn't come to an end, no one scolded her, and she was able to shrug off her parents' surprise without feeling as if she had let them down by her less-than-perfect performance. The pressure was lifting.

Even when she accepted her management position at the utility firm and was anxious to prove herself in the competitive corporate environment, she set limits for herself. She was willing to take on more than anyone else in the office, but she was also tuned into herself well enough to know when she had assumed her maximum workload.

"For instance, a couple of weeks ago my boss came in with yet another project for me. I already was working on six or seven. I realized that I very respectfully but firmly had to explain, 'I can't do any more right now.' Getting those words out wasn't easy, but I took a deep breath and said, 'Neal, you can give this job to me, but it won't get done for a couple of weeks because right now I have enough work to keep me busy non-stop until the first of the month.'"

His reaction?

"I don't know who was more surprised by my words—he or I. He sort of stammered around for a few seconds and finally agreed to give the project to someone else," said Judie. Then she laughed. "And me? I felt so good about myself that I smiled the rest of the day."

YEAH, YOU'RE OKAY; BUT THEN, SO AM I

Judie's experience is one we all can learn from. It contains layers of lessons. Of primary interest was that Judie learned that she couldn't please everyone.

That was Judie's problem, and it's the problem of most female over-achievers: They are so busy pleasing Mom and Dad, husband and children, boss and friends, they forget to consider the drain on themselves. One day they eventually wise up or wear out.

Judie learned to live with a *B* grade. If her parents had not been able to cope with that, who *really* would have needed help? Not Judie, that's for sure. She had learned two of life's basic rules:

1. Don't sweat the small stuff.
2. It's all small stuff.

Christ taught more by example than he did by lecture. He was an achiever, but not a workaholic. He focused on the things that mattered . . . *really* mattered; and he didn't worry about the opinions of others. Once, during a time of teaching, he was interrupted by someone in the crowd who said, "Your brothers and sisters are here to see you." His response was, "My family is made up of all these people around me" (see Luke 8:14-21).

When masses of people came forward for healing, Christ retreated to the mountains for rest and prayer. When messengers tried to pressure him to rush to the bed of his dying friend Lazarus, he finished his current ministry before moving on. His quiet confidence and steady competence helped him achieve amazing deeds while remaining serene and on-track for his chosen ministry.

And that's the secret. If your work—whether it is school work, family duties, community service, or a career—is done mainly to earn the applause of others, you've relinquished control of your life to those you are trying to please. You've cut a losing deal with everyone whose approval you crave. By your actions you've said to your spouse, to your parents, to your boss, or to your friends, "I'll do whatever is necessary to make you notice me, praise me, respect me, love me, admire me, applaud me. And if my actions become routine or predictable, I'll work harder to accomplish more so your applause will continue, or, better yet, grow in intensity. Just tell me what you want, and somehow I will deliver it."

When an over-achiever reaches this point she becomes like a performer who has neither director nor script. She responds eagerly—too eagerly—to the whims, demands, and expectations of her audience. She jumps, she spins, she dances on cue. She performs breathlessly, feeding on the accolades that her performance generates and whirling more and more out of control. The applause, like any other "high," becomes addictive. There's never quite enough to satisfy.

Sound uncomfortably familiar?

Dr. Robert Hemfelt, Dallas psychologist who specializes in treating driven people, says workaholism is degenerative. Left unchecked, it only gets worse. If it isn't confronted in its early stages, the tendency to achieve becomes an obsession to excel. The work steps up, but the applause dies down. The over-achiever misinterprets her audience's response to mean that the performance must have fallen short. Her remedy: She pushes even harder to regain the strokes that she needs.

Self-help begins with recognition and a commitment to change. Even if the "problem" is only a tendency, it needs to be seen for what it could become. The 12-Step Program, developed and used so successfully by members of Alcoholics Anonymous, is one way to begin any recovery process. It has been modified and utilized by such groups as Al-Anon, Overeaters Anonymous, Gamblers Anonymous,

Emotions Anonymous, and others. Simply put, it works. And it can work for women like us who are driven by the need to achieve.

12-STEP RECOVERY PROGRAM FOR OVER-ACHIEVERS

1. I realize that my drive for achievement is out of control.

2. I know that only God can put my life in balance.

3. I surrender my need to God.

4. As I look honestly at myself, I take stock of my strengths and my weaknesses.

5. I confess my mistakes to myself, to the people affected by my mistakes, and to God.

6. I prepare myself for God's forgiveness of my character flaws.

7. I pray to God that he will cleanse me of my short-comings.

8. I am aware of who has been hurt by my drivenness and I commit myself to finding ways to right those wrongs.

9. I face the people I have hurt and make restitution.

10. I judge my actions and when I falter I respond quickly and humbly to correct my errors.

11. As I work to strengthen my relationship with God I ask only to know his will for me.

12. My goal is to live my life according to God's plan and thereby to serve as an example for others.

THREE

Traits Shared, Games Played

Although most men talk about their wife's successful career with a great deal of pride, they may nevertheless associate her after-work hours with their care and comfort. Men still want to be nurtured.
—Nancy Collins, *Women Leading*

TIMES CHANGE. TERMS CHANGE.

Quickly.

In 1983 I wrote a book on workaholism. It became a best-seller. Five years later Hensley's view of workaholism was out of print. *Kaput,* and rightfully so. The information it contained was dated . . . out of step with contemporary thinking . . . outright wrong.

Was it because America had quit generating workaholics? Not at all. Each new phase of advanced technology had continued to produce the next bumper crop of fanatic devotees, all pledging their hours and lifetimes not only to building the better mousetrap, but also to springing it.

Like Holly's friend Judie in chapter two, they had become addicted to work at younger and younger ages.

It became faddish to be addicted to work. For that matter, it became faddish to be addicted to addictions of any sort. Alcoholics Anonymous no longer dominated the available retreat centers for self-confessed addicts. New support groups were formed with such apropos names as Over-eaters Anonymous, Shoplifters Anonymous, Sex Addicts Anonymous, even Spenders Anonymous (*Washington Times*, Feb. 6, 1989, p. E-2).

Barbara Hemphil, an efficiency expert, coined the term paperholics for people who never discard a check stub, college exam, or outdated fishing license. A popular tabloid reported that an attorney who suffered from paperholism was almost killed as a result of his addiction. In early 1989 the attorney was buried alive in his office when a wobbling stack of books and documents five feet high fell domino-style against several other equally high stacks of paper. In ten seconds the man found himself at the bottom of *five tons* of avalanched paper. It took rescue workers five hours to dig him out. Like this hapless attorney, many other people—especially women—felt as though the roof had fallen in on them during the late 1980s. Pressures had increased. They had to board the United jet, make the presentation, wow the client, and be back home in time to drive the second leg of the pre-school carpool. These women were labeled collec-tively as "workaholics."

"For me, a true workaholic is a combination of an over-achiever and a serious-contender rolled into one," says teacher and poet Mary Lou Carney. "She is intense and determined and competitive. This is what she *is*. It is not a role she assumes until the B.A. degree is completed or the car is paid for or the office with the window is acquired. It is a way of life, as much as the tilt of her nose. The woman who exerts a burst of determination to obtain a short-term goal is not an authentic workaholic. She is, truly, someone who is goal-oriented."

Florida-based novelist Jonellen Heckler, author of *White*

Lies, echoes this belief. "High achieving does not necessarily go with the word workaholic," says Jonellen. "The workaholic has things out of balance. I believe I am a high achiever but not a workaholic. I have priorities. I put my family first, but I also have a good career. I work on achieving balance."

Although a variety of terms have been coined to label workaholics, such as perfectionists, over-achievers, type-A personalities, and obsessive-compulsives ("o-c's" for short), in this book we will use the terms interchangeably. Instead of becoming bogged down in terminology of any sort, however, let's take time to follow the life of someone who evolved into a workaholic.

Sunny Bellamy was not a schizophrenic, but she had led two lives. And that is what had prompted her to ask for a chat session with me.

Sunny had read my book *Positive Workaholism* too late. She came across the book three years after her divorce had become final. She needed to talk with someone who would listen open-mindedly to her story and then tell her how she could have done things differently . . . or even *if* she could have done them differently. Her story provides us with an example of a woman's compulsive drive to achieve.

We met over coffee at a small restaurant in Portland, Oregon. I had told Sunny I had no sure-fire answers for people's problems, but she felt just having access to someone who had spent years researching the topic of workaholism would benefit her. So, I agreed to meet.

Her opening words were almost a cliche: "To look at me now, Dr. Hensley, you'd never guess that I was once an introverted, self-conscious, mousy little housewife whose only goals in life were to have a hot meal on the table when my husband arrived home at 5:30 and to be a good mom to my four children."

She was right. The woman across the table from me was anything but mousy. She was a youthful beauty who looked

35, despite the fact that her introductory letter had said she was 46. Her skin was tawny, as though she regularly spent time on the beach or a tanning bed. Her hair was deep black, fluffed full, and stylish. She wore makeup that accented her blue eyes and high cheekbones. Her clothes and jewelry were expensive. She sat poised and self-assured . . . yet somewhere behind her air of confidence I detected a hint of worry. Her appearance displayed boldness; her words suggested doubt. My curiosity was piqued.

"When I was growing up in Texas, I was a 'slow' child," she explained. "I couldn't tie my shoes until second grade. I was held back in fifth grade. Mother used to say to me, 'Learn to cook and clean house, Sunny, so you can get married. You're like I used to be. We may be short on brains, but we know how to keep our men happy. Once you get a ring on your finger, you don't have to worry.'

"I was pretty at fifteen and my mother nudged me faster and faster toward maturity. She gave me home perms every three months and showed me how to apply lipstick, rouge, and mascara. I felt awkward, like a six-year-old stumbling around in high heels playing dress up.

"Daddy got hurt one year and couldn't work. I became a waitress on weekends and after school at a truckstop two miles north of town. I came home in tears the first day and told Mama I'd never go back. The men called me 'honey' all day, and they patted my behind. Mama only chuckled and said men would be men and that they meant no harm and that if I'd play along with them, I'd get some good tips.

"I had plenty of boys ask me out. When I made it plain I didn't want sex, I seldom was asked out again. We attended a small church once a month, but more to scout available transient farm hands and wildcatters than to hear sermons. I always thought of myself as a good girl and I equated that with being a Christian. I sometimes even prayed that God would send a man my way."

Sunny fumbled in her purse a moment, located a photograph and pushed it across the table to me.

"When I was seventeen I met Jim Bellamy," she said, tapping the photo. "He was twenty-six. He had all that wavy hair and those beautiful teeth. He'd been in the army for three years and had recently started a heavy equipment and backhoe business in Oregon. He'd only been married two years when his wife suffered an asthma attack and suffocated. After a year as a widower Jim came to Texas to buy new equipment for his business and I met him at church. Mama arranged to invite him home for lunch and she made every effort to emphasize to him that I had made the delicious apple pie and I had canned the pickles and I had crocheted the doily and I had knitted the afghan.

"I should have been embarrassed, but for once, I was cheering Mama on. I wanted her to 'sell' me to this handsome businessman from Oregon. I cut Jim a second piece of *my* apple pie, scooped vanilla ice cream on it and served it to him. Jim asked Mama's permission to take me to dinner the next Friday and Mama flashed me a secret A-OK sign behind her back.

"Jim was only going to be in our area for three weeks. I took time off from my waitress job and we began to see each other every night—TV at home, the county fair, church on Wednesdays and Sundays, walks in the park, even a visit to my Aunt Julia's home. It was wonderful. Jim was patient, gentle, fun-loving, and completely open. When he told me how he had lost his wife, I cried. I admired him for the faithful relationship he had had with her. I never wanted him to lose the memory of their two sweet years together. I knew completely why Brenda had loved him so dearly. I was sure I would have, too.

"During my senior year Jim called me every weekend from Oregon and we wrote letters almost daily. He came to Texas at Christmas and in April. He proposed to me in April and I accepted before he even finished the sentence. I graduated in June and we were married a week later. When we boarded the train for Oregon, I was so happy I nearly fainted."

Sunny sipped her coffee, then continued her story. "I assume you thought your marriage to Jim would be all you needed out of life?"

Sunny nodded agreement.

"For a long time it was," she said. "When Jim was courting me, I told him I was just a hick kid from a small west-Texas town. I could cook, sew, put up preserves, hoe a garden, clean house, wash clothes, and tend children. Anything other than that, though, was beyond my capabilities. I wasn't smart enough for college or sophisticated enough to run a business."

"Did that disappoint Jim?"

"Not a bit," said Sunny. "It was exactly what he wanted to hear. He said he would be putting in a lot of hard hours for several years building his business and what he needed was a dependable wife who would be a lover and companion. He wanted me to look pretty and to make him the center of my attention for the rest of our lives. In return, he would be faithful to me and love me, and as he became more prosperous he would buy me nice things, take me on nice trips, and one day build me a mansion."

I smiled. "That sounds pretty ambitious for someone in his late twenties."

Sunny turned very serious. "Don't laugh," she warned. "Jim made good on every promise. He took me on vacation trips everywhere from Florida to Tahiti. He bought me new cars. And after we were married sixteen years he built us a huge house with a game room, five bathrooms, six bedrooms, a sundeck, a three-car garage, and a swimming pool."

I whistled low. "Wow! You really hitched your wagon to a rising star."

"Financially, yes," Sunny agreed, "but from an emotional

standpoint there was still a void in my life. No matter how many fur coats or diamond-studded watches Jim bought me . . . no matter how many trips we took . . . no matter how many children we had—two boys, two girls—I still had an emptiness within me. I once even had a bad dream about my sister mocking me and saying that I had acted like a tramp to get tips from the truckers and I was still acting like a tramp to get even nicer presents from Jim.

"But I had other dreams, too; really happy ones. I would dream of being back in grade school and hearing my teachers praise me for my special skills, like art and poetry. In those dreams I felt fulfilled. No longer was I the 'slow' child. Now I was the 'special' child, the 'gifted' one everyone watched in respect and amazement and—best of all—with envy. They wanted to be like me."

"Did you share those dreams and feelings with anyone else?" I asked.

"I tried one time," Sunny recalled. "We were back in Texas and Mama and I were up late one night talking about old times. I started telling Mama about my secret feeling of emptiness and I asked her advice about what to do. Her face turned panic-stricken, then angry. She warned me *never* to say anything to my good husband about any fool notion of emptiness and for me to count my lucky stars that a fine man like Jim Bellamy had made me his wife. She told me there were five hundred women waiting in line to live the way I did and that any talk of emptiness on my part was nothing short of ingratitude. After that, I never told anyone else about my secret feelings."

"What happened next?"

"For a couple of years we went along as usual," said Sunny. "Our children kept growing, Jim's business kept flourishing, and life was predictable but pleasant. Then in 1981 I started keeping a personal journal as a way of putting my emotions on paper and dealing with them in a private way. I was very honest about my joys, fears, and bewilderments. I kept the journal locked in a safe that had been installed to protect my jewelry.

"During the early years of our marriage Jim and I were active at a church near our home. As I spent more time reading my Bible and attending Sunday school classes, I realized that my childhood belief about 'being good' being the same as 'being a Christian' was not correct. I knelt at my home one morning after my private devotions and asked Christ to be my Savior. I asked for forgiveness of my past sins and for guidance in my new walk with him. I then *knew* I was a Christian because by then I knew what a Christian really was."

"That was quite an advancement in your spiritual growth," I said.

"Yes, but it also created new problems for me," said Sunny. "It made me accountable to God's laws and his plan for the family. I loved my children and I was tremendously fond of Jim. But in my secret journal I confessed that I was facing a great dilemma. When I had married Jim, I had been sure that my marriage would be the thing that would make me feel like the 'special' person I longed to be. If Jim could do that for me, I would love him immeasurably for the rest of my life. I would have no problem being submissive to a man who made me feel complete, fulfilled, unique."

Sunny lowered her head and avoided my gaze. "But there's where the dilemma arose," she added. "After twenty years of marriage, I still felt unfulfilled. Jim had given me money, security, children, a home. He'd kept or exceeded all his promises to me, yet he'd failed to help me discover in myself something uniquely mine, something I could feel special about. And because he had failed at that, the rest really didn't matter much to me."

"Did Jim know how you felt?" I asked.

"No. I kept up the act. Why not? He worked hard every day and he was utterly in love with me. So, I still served him homemade apple pie with a scoop of vanilla ice cream. It wasn't hypocritical, really. He *was* my husband and he *did* deserve my best. But even good sex and good companionship couldn't quite meet that particular need I still felt inside in me.

"After twenty years it had tripled in size. We had new friends, new avenues of fellowship, new ways of serving the Lord. Then one Sunday morning, quite by accident, my life was changed. Our associate pastor was leaving for a two-week vacation. He needed someone to assemble the news for our monthly church newsletter, type it, get it copied and mailed. His secretary would be available if a volunteer needed assistance. So, I volunteered."

Sunny smiled, then continued, "When I came to the church on Monday to assemble the news items and type them, the secretary told me I'd also need to write a three hundred-word article for the newsletter's back page. I tried to protest that I had never claimed to be a writer. She laughed and said, 'Just share your thoughts about anything special to you. Maybe something about your family. A few hundred words won't be that hard. Try it.'

"I spent the morning typing the other news items, but a half-page of blank space on the back page reminded me I had to come up with some kind of an article. I drove home at noon but had no appetite for lunch. I pulled out my journals hoping to get an idea. After several minutes of flipping pages, I discovered something that had potential.

"A year earlier our family had taken a vacation by car to Seattle. As we were set to pull out of the driveway, my husband asked our younger daughter Ellen to pray for us. Ellen thanked God for our health, our family love, and our opportunity to enjoy this vacation. She then stunned us with, 'And, Lord, I pray that all the travelers on the road today will have safe journeys. But if accidents do have to happen and people do have to die today, please let it be members of our family. We are saved and are ready to be with you in heaven. Other people may still be lost in sin and may need more time to know Jesus Christ. I will gladly give up my life if it means a lost soul will have the opportunity to be saved.'

"The power and strength of my daughter's faith had humbled me that day. I had noted her prayer in my journal. Now I decided to share it in the church newsletter. The article practically wrote itself. It actually ran 325 words, but I was able to squeeze it all into the newsletter. I took the master copy of the newsletter to a print shop, had 175 copies made and then I put labels on them. By 6 P.M. everything was finished and mailed. I felt relieved.

"By 10:00 the next morning my phone started ringing. Our senior pastor had read a copy of the newsletter. He called to say that my article was the most gripping short devotional he'd ever read. He asked me to write a column every month in the newsletter. I was flabbergasted. *Me? A columnist? A writer?* No, no, surely not.

"Yet, even as I was protesting, something inside me was saying, 'This is it! This is it! This is the self-fulfillment you've been searching for.' So, I amazed even myself by telling the pastor I would try my hand at writing the column.

"As soon as I hung up, the phone rang again. It was my neighbor, Louise. She was crying. She told me she had just received her newsletter and my article about Ellen's prayer had moved her to tears. She said she was going to cut it out and tape it to the dashboard of her family's car. She then said, 'I hope you'll write other things, Sunny. You really have a gift.'

"Again I was stunned. I had never considered myself talented—gifted—at writing. Nevertheless, as the phone calls continued to come in, I found myself truly reveling in my new-found identity as a writer. I pulled out my journal and began to search for another idea. I came across an observation I had once made about how the autumn changing of tree leaf colors reminded me of the beauty all things—especially people—can have in the last phases of life. I started writing a column about that.

"While working on my second column, I received a call from the editor of our denomination's national magazine. He wanted to reprint my newsletter item and offered me $75 for one-time publication rights. Someone actually wanted to *pay* me to be a writer. If ever there was confirmation of my 'gift,' this was it.

"During those early weeks of my budding writing career my family was ecstatic about my success. Jim noticed how much happier I seemed to be, so when he saw a little newspaper item about a writer's conference in Seattle, he clipped it and put it on my dressing table. He said I would learn more about the business end of writing as well as increase my skills. So, I went. While at the conference I set a goal for myself: to become so successful as a writer, one day I would be invited to teach at a writer's conference just like the successful writers who were our teachers that week.

"I came home all fired up. For three months I virtually lived at the typewriter. I wrote twelve short columns for our church newsletter and turned them in all at once. I sent copies of all twelve columns to our denominational magazine. The editor rejected six, but accepted the other six and sent me a check for $400. This was more money than I used to earn in a month as a truck-stop waitress.

"Each time I saw my name in print, it stimulated me, made me feel excited, wonderful, alive, important . . . but it also made me want more. To feed my ego habit, I spent more and more time at the typewriter. Meals became sandwiches quickly slapped together. I skipped PTA meetings, Wednesday night prayer meetings, office parties at my husband's business, visits with my neighbors. My mother wanted to know why I kept the phone answering machine on all day long. My husband wondered if I was ever going to come to bed at night with him. One of my children joked that there was so much dust on our furniture, someone should plant a crop. After awhile, however, the jokes weren't funny.

"At first I laughed with them about their inconveniences. As the complaints continued, though, I became bitter. I told them my writing was important. I was earning good money which we could use for a better life. And I was helping people with my articles. Jim responded that we didn't need a second income and that if I wanted to help people I could start at home by washing some dishes and baking a homemade apple pie and attending a Little League game.

"In my air of rebellion, I refused to yield to these demands. I continued to write articles and columns and submit them to a wide range of Christian and secular magazines. Things grew worse at home, but I didn't care. I lived for the next byline, the next royalty check, the next acceptance letter, the next word of praise from a reader.

"Perhaps I was overreacting. But in a real sense I was running scared. Freelance writing, I discovered, was ruled by deadlines, stress, pressure of all sorts. I was also afraid of rumors I'd heard. Someone had said that if you ever turned down an assignment offer from an editor, you'd never get another chance to work for that person. As a result, I never said no.

"I probably would have continued this breakneck pace had it not been for a small, innocent, but very honest scene that transpired one October morning. I had worked all night trying to finish a sample chapter for a book proposal I wanted to submit to a New York publisher. At 5 A.M. my daughter Ellen came wandering through our house looking for me. She'd had a nightmare and needed a hug. I paused a minute from my typing to give her a squeeze and to assure her that she would be fine.

"As I was just about to shoo her back to bed, Ellen looked at me and said 'You look sick, Mommy. Your eyes look funny. Are you sick, Mommy?' I was taken aback by this. *My eyes? Sick?* What was she talking about?

"I walked into the bathroom and took a serious look at myself. I was shocked at what I saw. My eyes *did* look funny. They were bloodshot, deeply red and lined with dark veins. My eye sockets were black, sunken, and hollow. My hair wasn't styled and it had not been touched up for months, causing it to look streaked and flecked with grey and white. I wasn't wearing makeup. My teeth looked stained. I was wearing a Snoopy teeshirt I'd had on for three days. I couldn't believe what I saw. I had always been meticulous about my grooming. Now, I looked like . . . what? . . . an addict! I sat on the edge of the bathtub and cried for half an hour. What had I done? What had I become? I couldn't believe I'd gotten so out of control. I had to stop. I knew I needed to get my perspective on things again.

"I pulled myself together, went to the kitchen, put on a pot of coffee and began to fry bacon and eggs and to make fresh biscuits. By 6 A.M. the smells of hot food brought everyone to the table. Jim hugged me when he saw the breakfast and the kids told me how good things tasted. It was like the old days. I had a feeling it wasn't too late to change.

"After everyone left for the morning, I went to bed and slept until noon. I then got up, made a casserole for dinner and spent the afternoon cleaning house and catching up on laundry. Before Jim came home I took a shower, fixed my hair and makeup, put on a favorite dress, and had iced tea and a pre-dinner snack ready for him when he arrived. Jim came in with flowers for me. Things seemed so normal again. We were back on track. We all had dinner together and the conversation was noisy and excited. There was a feeling around the table that a celebration was taking place. The prodigal Mom had returned.

"I kept so busy during the day I hadn't thought about my pending writing projects. That night, however, when Jim and I were in bed, I found myself thinking again about the book proposal even as Jim was kissing me. I assured myself that in time I would reduce my passion for writing and revive my passion for Jim.

"During the next ten days I had fun. I went to the beauty parlor and I shopped for new clothes and I met a friend for lunch downtown. I continued to write for two hours in the afternoon. I convinced myself this would be enough. And it actually might have been enough, had two things not happened.

"In mid-November I was sitting at my kitchen table going over a menu for a big Thanksgiving dinner, the doorbell rang. I was asked to sign for an overnight Express Mail delivery. The return address was from the New York publisher I had submitted my book proposal to. I held my breath, opened the envelope, then screamed. It was an offer to publish my book. All I had to do was deliver a completed manuscript by February 15.

"Immediately my old enthusiasm came back. I wanted to see my name on a book. If I could do that, then I'd stop. I'd be fulfilled. Just one book. Surely Jim and the kids wouldn't begrudge me this. It was *all* I wanted.

"I practically ran to my writing room. Minutes later, in the middle of organizing notes, pulling out research files, and putting paper into the typewriter, I had to stop to answer the phone. I had forgotten to turn on the answering machine. I went to the kitchen and grabbed up the receiver. I would quickly get rid of whoever it was.

" 'Mrs. Bellamy? Sunny Bellamy?'

" 'Yes,' I answered. 'Who's calling?'

" 'This is Glenda DeWitt. I'm director of the Far Oaks, California writer's conference. Would you be available to be one of our guest lecturers this next June? I've read several of your articles. I'm sure our attendees would enjoy hearing your secrets of success as a writer.' "

Sunny paused in her narrative. She sipped her coffee,

shrugged her shoulders, then looked at me resolutely.

"You can guess the rest," she said slowly. "I went right back to my old ways. My family felt betrayed. Everyone complained. I insisted my writing was a ministry. Nobody empathized with me. I retaliated by not telling anyone about the writer's conference or about an offer to write a sequel to my first book. The only one I punished by this, however, was me. Nobody else in the family *wanted* to hear about my writing.

"I began to accept more offers to lecture. I was away from home more than I was at home. I once came home a day earlier than expected and no one was around. They had all gone on an overnight camp outing. They had learned to go on with their lives without me.

"I actually thought this was great. I had gotten to the point where I wanted a family, but just so long as nobody got in my way, disrupted my routine, or put any demands on me. Soon, Jim carried this to extreme measures. He filed for divorce. I thought he was joking. He was serious. And the worst part was that the kids wanted to stay with him."

I interrupted, "Did you seek help from a counselor?"

Sunny nodded yes. "At our third session with the counselor I told her that I wasn't the woman Jim had married years ago. Jim countered by saying that I should go back to my old self. I vowed I never would. The next day I, too, hired a lawyer. The divorce was final five months later."

"And what about your life since then?"

"Ups and downs," admitted Sunny. "Jim kept the house and business. I received a $35,000 settlement. That carried me for about three years. But now, instead of getting to work, I *have* to work. It's not the same. I've written five books and I get to travel a lot. I like that very much. But I live alone and my apartment is modest and my children don't visit me very often. Jim has remarried. His new wife is a nobody compared to my status as a national celebrity, but she's ten years younger than I am and very pretty and at times it angers me to think that Jim could be happier with her than he was with me."

"Was it worth it?" I ventured. "You know . . . the divorce? The career?"

Again Sunny shrugged her shoulders. "Ask me that during the middle of an autograph party or just before a TV talk show appearance and I'll say yes in an instant. But ask me when I'm alone on my birthday or when there's no one to snuggle up to in bed at night or when I'm trimming the Christmas tree by myself, and I'll say no. A better question is, could I have done it differently? I know that there are women out there who manage to balance a family life and a career. I keep wondering why I couldn't, too."

Sunny's story ended on a bittersweet note of success and failure. Versions of it can be heard all over America. Women want a change in their lives, yet they also want to maintain the status quo of what they already have. Somehow they feel that this is possible if they just work longer and harder. They sometimes become so addicted to this new treadmill existence, they can never turn it off again. As one researcher has reported recently, not even divorce can stop it once it becomes a part of a woman's self-identity.

"Divorce itself inevitably changes you," writes California psychologist Diane Medved in *The Case Against Divorce* (David Fine Publishers, 1989). "Divorce diminishes your moral perspective; it staggers you emotionally for months and years; it forces a change in your home and living standards; and it eliminates the friendships of half the names in your address book. Still, there are some things, unfortunately, that it does not automatically affect: the patterns in your behavior that led to your marital problems in the first place."

Sunny Bellamy would be the first to admit this. Her life was radically altered after her divorce, yet her workaholic tendencies stayed at the same high level. Her justification for this used to be the demands of editors and the necessity to meet deadlines. Now her justification is the need to earn a living. But if a long-lost relative died tomorrow and left Sunny a fortune, she'd just find another justification to keep working so hard: "I'm fulfilling my ministry" . . . "I need to try new things if I'm ever going to grow as a writer" . . . "Writing keeps my mind off my other problems." Diane Medved is right when she says women like Sunny don't easily alter their workaholic behavior patterns.

How do these women become this way? For many, like Sunny, it is a desperate need for love that somehow gets out of control and becomes egocentric self-aggrandizement. These women are not out to revolutionize the world. They just want to turn the focus of the world—on them. They are not leaders of movements, they are what is known as quiet rebels.

"The quiet rebel who seeks to change attitudes toward herself and the way she is treated will probably be motivated by purely personal concerns," writes Dr. Glynis Breakwell in *The Quiet Rebel: How to Survive as a Woman and Businessperson* (Grove Press, 1985). "She wants to be allowed to pursue her chosen career to the best of her ability. Any changes she may induce will be brought about for her personal advantage. By definition, the quiet rebel is not interested in the position of women; she is interested in *her own* position. Social change is not her objective; personal advancement is" (p. 194).

This is not to say, however, that all highly motivated women who seek to have a career must expect to become uncontrollable workaholics who will eventually wind up in divorce court. Steps can be taken to inject the "balance" Sunny Bellamy so desperately desired yet never found.

Her family *first demanded* that she put her roles as wife and mother before all else. When she found this impossible to continue (after eighteen years of doing it) *then* she wanted them to agree to accept her *new* roles. Some compromises would have been in order.

In thinking back on Sunny's story it becomes quickly obvious that much more could have been done on Jim's part. His very traditional way of assuming that his needs were of more importance than Sunny's is not uncommon of many men of his era. Even worse, he was unable to see that what may have been right for his relationship with Sunny at the start of their marriage might not have been at all appropriate two decades later. Times change and so do people. Needs change, too.

When Sharon and Tim Mowrer of Fort Wayne, Indiana, were first married, they were content to live in a small home and let Tim be the primary breadwinner. In short order, however, their goals changed. They wanted a family, a better home, a second car, and nice furniture. So, Sharon took a job (part-time and temporary) as a secretary. They did not intend for her to work out of the home once they started a family.

After the first and second babies arrived, the Mowrers had to reassess their earlier feelings about a "working mom." They both still wanted to enjoy the earning power Sharon had, yet they felt they needed to spend quality time together as a family. They had several talks about the matter and it was Tim who suggested they form a partnership. Sharon could continue to be a typist and bookkeeper, but she would start her own business working out of their home. Tim could help with bookkeeping and accounting duties for clients during Sharon's busiest seasons (tax time and quarterly inventories). Tim kept his salaried job and Sharon built her business into a successful operation. She still had time to do half of the school car pool duties and she was at home when the kids came in from school. It was not the life Tim and Sharon had assumed they would be leading when they first married, but it was one just as full and enjoyable.

Despite Tim Mowrer's willingness to work with his wife

in making her career something of equal value to his, recent research shows that there is some "merit" in the "outdated" beliefs of men like Jim Bellamy. A 1990 study titled, "Through the Eyes of Children: Parental Roles in Contemporary Families," examined one hundred twenty-one four-year-olds enrolled in out-of-home child care programs in Indianapolis and Muncie. The study found that sixty-two percent of the children saw caregiving as a mother's role, eighteen percent saw it as a father's role, and the remaining twenty percent saw it as a shared role.

The study, which was conducted by Judith E. Stroud and Ena M. Goodrich-Shelley of Butler University and James C. Stroud of Ball State University, focused on twenty-one children being raised by single fathers, fifty by single mothers, and fifty by married couples. Each child had no older brothers or sisters who might have influenced his thinking.

The researchers presented the children with twenty-four pictures representing domestic life: washing dishes, carrying out the garbage, giving the baby a bath, running the vacuum cleaner, making beds, and cooking dinner. The children said that changing diapers and doing the laundry and keeping house were "Mommy's jobs," whereas going to the ballgame, watching television with the kids, washing the car, and cutting the grass were "Daddy's jobs." Since it is hard to accuse a four-year-old of stereotyping, these findings indicate there may be a feeling that is either innate in humans about what female roles should be *or* that women are better than men at performing homecare duties. Even in homes where fathers did as much cooking and housekeeping as their spouses, the children still saw those duties as more the responsibility of the mother than the father. (So much for the excuse from husbands who won't do housework because it presents the wrong "role model" for their children.)

Here are some guidelines:

1. Spend time in prayer every day, not just alone but also with your spouse and children. See that you are honest with

God and your loved ones. Being honest with your loved ones will help them understand and support you, afford them the opportunity to grow with you, and work to give you the space you need to explore new avenues without leaving them behind. Ask your family to pray for you to receive God's guidance in your work and ministry.

2. Don't take everything in life so seriously. George MacDonald once wrote, "It is the heart that is unsure of his God that is afraid to laugh." William Barclay reminded us, "It must never be forgotten that joy is one of the commonest New Testament words." If problems arise between you and your spouse (or your boss, your kids, your friends), ask yourself how important this matter will be six months from now. If you can, laugh rather than cry; smile rather than frown; encourage rather than criticize. Proverbs 15:26 tells us that "the words of the pure are pleasant words."

3. Try to separate your career achievements (or setbacks) from your identity as a human being. In this way, if you receive great praise for something you have done, you will not become egotistical. Similarly, if you have a career setback, you will not feel as though you have lost your priceless value to your family.

Sunny's problem was that she began to think that her career *was* her life. To her way of thinking, if she failed to please an editor, she'd fail to get her articles in print. That, in turn, would cost her the readership following she had developed. People would forget her. She would become a nobody again and this would embarrass her family. This, of course, was nonsense; but it seemed very real to Sunny.

Christian counselors Dennis and Barbara Rainey of Little Rock, Arkansas, explain, "Most women don't realize they can fail and not be a failure. They haven't learned to separate their personal worth from their career performance. These women find it difficult to have their ideas, work, or goals criticized because they feel they, personally, are being criticized and rejected. If they can once get past that, life becomes far less of a burden to them."

One of the most important truths that frees us to accept failure is the fact that God loves us. It's his love and acceptance that enable us to fail and not consider ourselves failures. Before God our primary value is not in what we do but who we are—his daughter, made in his image, inherently valuable.

4. Seek areas of commonalities rather than emphasizing career differences. It may take some effort to discover ways in which your work and your husband's work can be overlapped, but it can be done. Sunny made the mistake of making her husband feel like an outsider to her work as a writer. Jim *wanted* to be a helper. He was the one who suggested the writer's conference to Sunny. Sunny, however, wanted all the glory for herself. She should have shared the joy of her work with Jim.

My coauthor Holly Miller and her husband Phil have very divergent careers. Holly is a college professor and author, whereas Phil is an executive with a manufacturing plant that specializes in building recreational equipment. He is also a part-time student pursuing a doctoral degree in management. You would think there would be no common ground in their careers, right? Well, they sought out and found common ground.

Phil proofreads Holly's book manuscripts and offers his views on subjects she is researching; he attends writers' conferences where she is a guest instructor and helps pass out handout materials or set up the A-V equipment; he enjoys attending plays or concerts with Holly when she must attend as a reviewer and critic. Equally supportive, Holly frequently goes by Phil's office to drop off a milkshake and just check up on things: she really *knows* about Phil's work. She attends social and educational functions with Phil that are related to post-graduate courses he is taking. She talks with him about his classes and plays devil's advocate when he's brainstorming ideas for term papers or research topics. She likes to hear about his projects at the office. Now that both of Phil and Holly's sons are grown and living away from home, this couple has no problem with the empty nest syndrome. Why should they? They are living together as a married couple and as good friends.

Proverbs 5:18 says to "rejoice with the wife of thy youth." That goes two ways. A woman needs to rejoice, *i.e.*, share her work and dreams and fun times with the husband she has had since her youth, too. Draw closer with passing years, not farther apart.

FOUR

Bucking the Mara Myth

When you cease to make a contribution, you begin to die.
—Eleanor Roosevelt, 1960

YOU REMEMBER MARA.

Only you probably know her better as Naomi, wife of Elimelech, mother of Mahlon and Chilion, and mother-in-law of Ruth and Orpah. And that was her problem.

Naomi made the mistake of defining *who* she was by *what* she did, a practice some of us women still follow today. Naomi didn't see herself merely as Naomi. Instead, she was Naomi-wife-of-Elimelech-and-mother-of-Mahlon-and-Chilion-and-mother-in-law-to-Ruth-and-Orpah. What a mouthful! But she loved every breathless syllable. She believed that her identity was established by the qualifiers that followed her name. Her worth came from the words between the hyphens. Her value as a person was all confused with her work as a wife, mother, and mother-in-law. Her significance was determined by her job, and her job—like the jobs of most Old Testament women—was caring for her family. Without her family and her work, she believed she was nothing.

In Naomi's eyes, when her husband and two sons died in

Moab she lost her reason for living. She suffered a sort of deep depression that was obvious to her former neighbors as soon as they greeted her on her return to Bethlehem.

Picture the homecoming: Naomi, who had been gone several years, arrived on the scene with her beautiful daughter-in-law, Ruth. The women of Bethlehem gathered, anticipating the hugs, smiles, and animated girl talk that usually accompanied such a reunion. Instead, the celebration was tainted by Naomi's intense melancholy.

"Is it really Naomi?" the women of Bethlehem asked, marveling at the unexpected return of their dear friend.

Naomi brushed them away, telling them not to call her by her former name because Naomi meant "pleasant," and that certainly didn't describe the way she felt.

"Call me Mara," she insisted. Translated, "mara" was the word for "bitter," and "bitter" better suited her state of mind. "I went out full, and the Lord has brought me home empty," she complained (Ruth 1:18-21, *The Living Bible*).

If we read her words carefully, we know that Naomi/Mara was mourning much more than the loss of her husband and sons. She was mourning the loss of her identity and her self-esteem. They were intertwined in an all-or-nothing kind of package. Without her family she was without value.

We still see this happening today, and not just among widows. Reverend Don Hawkins, former executive director of the Minirth-Meier counseling clinic in Dallas, Texas, believes everyone has three basic needs in life—intimacy with God, intimacy with other people, and a feeling of self worth. These needs are closely related since intimacy with God and warm relationships with other people can help us feel loved, accepted, and needed. They can boost our self worth. But for some high-achievers, such intimacies are difficult to establish. Instead, their self-esteem is tightly linked to their careers or their work as wives and mothers. They need their roles to affirm their worth.

In his book *Creating a Lifestyle You Can Live With*, Dr. Ron

Fronk notes, "Low self-esteem is definitely one of our nation's biggest problems. Little wonder—from birth we're taught that our value comes from what we do and what we have rather than from who we are" (Whitaker House, 1988, p. 243). Radio psychologist Dr. Joy Browne echoes these ideas when she writes about women who work outside the home. "Work has become so intimately tied with status, women seem to have acquired the tendency to define themselves in terms of the work they do. . . . A capitalistic society has done its work and convinced both sexes that we are worth as much as we get paid for" (*Nobody's Perfect*, Simon and Schuster, 1988, p. 283).

Of course, the whole issue of people over-identifying with work isn't new, and it can't be blamed on "our nation," as Fronk claims, or on a "capitalistic society" as Browne believes. It's much older than that. Again, remember Naomi. In her case she knew that she was too old to remarry or have children; and, without children, what purpose did she have? The sorrow that engulfed her shortly after the deaths of her husband and sons had been replaced by anger and bitterness. The anger was directed at God. She blamed him not only for taking her family, but also for replacing busy, happy Naomi with empty, bitter Mara.

But Naomi's story had a happy ending of sorts. We know that Ruth, the faithful daughter-in-law who traveled with Naomi to Bethlehem, followed her mother-in-law's advice and married a wealthy relative. This not only assured Ruth's happiness, but it also reinstated Naomi's worth. With the marriage came a baby, and with the baby came a purpose for Naomi. Ruth had a son and Naomi had a job. Her assignment as nurse for the child gave her a reason to exist. Once again she had identity. Suddenly she was Naomi-mother-in-law-of-Ruth-and-grandmother-of-Obed. Meaningful qualifiers followed her name. There was life between those hyphens.

As the women of Bethlehem celebrated the baby's arrival,

they also cheered the return of their old, dear friend. "He shall be unto thee a restorer of thy life," they predicted. Goodbye, Mara. Welcome back, Naomi.

Happy ending? Well, yes. At least for Naomi's day it was. But her day was an era when women couldn't vote or own property or serve in government or enlist in the military or do much of anything except serve the needs of their families. Today, however, we live in a time when women have more choices about career and service. One would think it would be impossible for any woman of the twentieth century to say, "call me Mara." But millions are saying it every day. Unfortunately, the problem is still with us.

I AM WHAT I DO

These days we call it the empty-nest syndrome. It's what every mother feels after she helps her kindergarten-bound "baby" onto the school bus for the first time and then goes into the kitchen to celebrate her freedom with a good cry. It's why we sniffle at graduations, dab our mascara at weddings, and complain that we have something in our eye at the precise moment our teenage daughter models her first pair of high heels. Like Mara, we mourn the loss of those qualifiers after our names. Our role as parents is to make our children self-sufficient and independent. We "succeed" as we make ourselves more and more nonessential. However, self worth sometimes dips when we work ourselves out of these parenting jobs.

I suppose everyone has a Naomi in her life. Mine is named Joyce, a sturdy, practical type who came highly recommended as a role model when I joined my husband's family twenty-five years ago. Cousin Joyce had all the answers even before I knew what questions to ask. A regular Heloise, she could organize a kitchen, balance the household books, and turn her husband's collars to double the life of his shirts.

And she seemed to do it all simultaneously. A human octopus! For her, fixing dinner was a process. For me, it was a production. She did it by steps, I did it by whim. My idea of taking a night off was to send out for pizza. Hers was to skimp on one of the four basic food groups.

I used to worry that I tried her patience. I later learned that I gave her purpose. In those early months of my marriage I became one of a string of qualifiers after her name. She was Joyce—Mom, mate, mentor, and role model. In her eyes, she *was* what she *did*.

Like Naomi, Joyce eventually suffered a major upheaval in her life that changed her personality and frightened everyone who loved her. We should have seen it coming. Her friends—and that includes me—should have known something was wrong when she began losing too much weight too quickly. At first she looked good, and then she looked gaunt. She didn't smile as often, her phone calls to us tapered off, and gradually she withdrew from social commitments. "Where's Joyce?" we'd ask. *Busy,* we assumed. Joyce had always been busy. So we lost touch. Then one day we heard that Joyce was being counseled for severe depression.

"Joyce?" we asked incredulously. Steady, reliable, I've-got-everything-under-control *Joyce*? For the first time that I could remember, Joyce needed us more than we needed her. And that was her problem.

The similarities with Naomi were remarkable. If only we had remembered Mara, we might have been less shocked by what was happening to Joyce. Not that her three children had died, of course; they had simply grown up. Within a short time one had gone off to college, a second had begun his senior year of high school, and the third was waiting tables on weekends in order to finance a car. Joyce had simply worked herself out of a job. The list of qualifiers after her name had been trimmed, and in her eyes her value had been trimmed as well.

If Joyce's condition was similar to Naomi's, so was her

cure. At her counselor's suggestion, she and her husband became foster parents to what child welfare agencies categorize as "hard-to-place" children. These are school-age kids with problems. They need a mom, a mentor, and a role model. Joyce fit the job description perfectly. She had had plenty of experience. She and her husband ended up adopting three of the children whom they cared for as foster parents. Suddenly the nest was full again and Joyce had a meaningful mission. There was identity among those hyphens once more. Her smile returned, phone contact was reestablished, her schedule picked up, and she even gained weight.

WHY DO YOU PUSH SO HARD?

That question was at the heart of a survey I distributed among dozens of women in preparation for this book. In addition to soliciting written responses, I followed up with several personal interviews, conducted either on the phone, face-to-face over coffee, or through the long (and often slow) process of correspondence.

I met with some resistance. A few women took issue with the term "workaholic"; it was too negative, they said, because it brought to mind single-focused, out-of-balance malcontents. It was a label that they certainly would never apply to themselves. However, they liked "high-achiever," and, after some thought, ranked "over-achiever" someplace in between.

Other women expressed honest fear that they were on the debilitating course that moves from high-achiever to over-achiever to workaholic. Where's the line? they wondered. When does enthusiasm for good performance become a preoccupation and eventually an obsession with perfection? Is there a way to know where each of us fits into the spectrum?

I had asked many of these same questions in my interviews with psychologists. I had been told that there are several "indicators" that can help a high-achiever know if she has crossed the threshhold from a healthy attitude toward work to an unhealthy preoccupation with performance. For instance, she can:

—Keep an hourly log of daily activities. At the end of a week, tally the hours spent in major activities. Note if one activity is dominating your day to the exclusion of others.

—Draw two pie charts, one based on your typical week day and the second based on your typical Saturday. Divide the pie according to how much time is occupied by your various roles as a: parent, wife, volunteer, homemaker, worker, friend, daughter. Is any role obviously being neglected?

—Make a list of all your important relationships—with your spouse, children, neighbors, parents, friends, associates. Ask yourself, Are any of these relationships being shortchanged because of my preoccupation with achievement?

Like my cousin Joyce, many of the women I surveyed were homemakers; others worked in various professions out of the home. Regardless of work status or family situation, the women responded with answers that indicated there's a lot of Naomi in all of us. *What* they did— whether it was practicing law, teaching college classes or Sunday school, caring for children, volunteering countless hours to community service—wasn't nearly as important as *why* they did it with such gusto.

Let me explain.

To help prod answers from the women I contacted, I listed a string of possible responses to my point-blank question, "What is your primary motivation for working as hard as you do?" Is it money? Recognition? A sense of importance? I separated the answers according to whether the respondents were career women or homemakers. I fully expected the women who worked out of the home to claim money as their primary driver. But I was wrong. The overwhelming majority of all the women, career women and homemakers alike, said they worked for "personal satisfaction." The second more common motive for work was "creative outlet" followed by a "sense of importance."

These women affirmed what Dr. Marilyn Machlowitz wrote several years ago: "To most workaholics, psychic income—that is, responsibility, meaning, opportunity, recognition—seems more important than financial income" (Machlowitz, *Workaholics: Living with Them, Working with Them*, Mentor Books, 1981, p. 123).

Though this "psychic income" is so vital, it doesn't come without a price. "What sacrifices have you made?" I asked the sample of high-achieving women who filled out my questionnaire. "What have you given up in return for this personal satisfaction, creative outlet, and sense of importance?" Their answers ranged from cute to candid to painful. Among the more playful: "Sleep!" "A 'spotless' house." "Time to goof off." "Romance novels." "My 'soaps,' but don't tell anyone that I used to watch them." Then there were the answers so honest that they were almost painful to read. These were the replies that filled the margins, spilled over onto the back pages, required attached memos and extra sheets of note paper to complete.

• "I don't know what 'quiet' is, and I hope I never find out," scribbled a hospital pink lady whose record number of service hours had earned her certificates, pins, and the designation as Volunteer of the Year for four successive years. "I got involved after my husband was hospitalized with terminal colon cancer in 1985. When he died, my grief was so overwhelming that I could hardly function. His illness had totally occupied me for months; now I had an enormous void in my life. I found that by keeping busy at the hospital I didn't have time to cry or, for that matter, even to *think!* The more noise and activity, the better. The trouble is, I've noticed that now I don't like to be alone even for an evening. I get depressed and sort of weepy. It scares me. I know women who crave solitude. But me? It's become my worst enemy."

● "What have I sacrificed?" repeated a successful government employee who is known for her marathon workdays. "Emotional well-being, I'd say. That is, at times I have felt guilty because I've neglected certain important areas in my life. Like relationships . . . family. This always happens when I try to juggle too many projects."

● "I've made four big trade-offs," replied a middle-aged office manager. "First, my marriage, although the job wasn't entirely to blame. Second, some quality time with my daughter, although working has afforded us many opportunities, monetary, and otherwise. Third, time to myself, although my job *does* force organization. Fourth, a certain degree of stress, although *not* working causes me frustration and I'm not sure which is worse—stress or frustration."

Other comments:

● "I don't do *anything* as well as I'd like to."

● "I don't 'do lunch.' I have few truly close friends. I simply don't take the time to make them. If it doesn't involve my family, I don't do it. I shop from catalogs, never watch TV, take part in only selected church activities, never clip coupons or try new recipes or read women's magazines."

● "I think my kids missed out on a lot of things because I was so interested in being out of the house. They missed some guidance they could have had along the way. I never gave them the 'third degree' on what they did each day because I had other things to talk about, think about, and worry about. But some good came from this; they're very independent today. They don't need me at all."

Don't misunderstand me. I'm not rapping the knuckles of these women who admit to making sacrifices. I like their honesty, I relate to their answers, and I understand the feelings behind their responses. Trade-offs, sacrifices, and compromises come with high-achievement. But when pre-occupation with perfection in one area wins out too often over other obligations, problems can result.

Satisfaction? Creative outlet? Psychic income? Getting more than mere money or enjoyment from any task is terrific—a real bonus—unless the situation becomes as negative as the one described by the author of Ecclesiastes when he pessimistically wrote, "There is *nothing better* for men than that they should be happy in their work, for that is what they are here for, and no one can bring them back to life to enjoy what will be in the future, so let them enjoy it now" (Ecclesiastes 3:22).

Nothing better than satisfying work? Certainly work shouldn't be viewed as drudgery or as a necessary evil. But neither should it be an escape from or a substitute for a rich family and spiritual life. Balance is everything.

I am intrigued by the trends that indicate that the amount of leisure time for the average American has shrunk by a third; that the modern woman's work week has stretched to 52.2 hours; that career women in the United States spend fifty percent more time working on Saturdays now than they did twenty years ago; and that Americans, in general, put in an average of two hours of labor on Sundays!

What intrigues me about these statistics is that no one knows exactly how to interpret them. On the one hand, they could represent the most negative aspects of family disunity—Mom is never home on weekends anymore; we've forgotten how to "play" as a family; Sunday has become just another workday. On the other hand, this research could just as easily be showing that our society is closer now to fulfilling the lesson of Ecclesiastes 3:22 than ever before—we love our occupations and preoccupations so much that our work *is* our play; we have discovered that satisfying work, whatever it may be, can continue on weekends thanks to the telephone, worldwide computer linkups, after-hours bank machines, fax transmitters, answering machines, and other technological innovations that are not restricted to a traditional five-day work week.

Perhaps even a third speculation is plausible: Maybe we don't know what the research means and maybe *we don't care* to know. Work? Play? Do we even need a distinction? John P. Robinson, director of the Americans' Use of Time Project, says that many people are fuzzy on the issue of which way they most like to spend their hours—at work or at leisure. "When asked to choose whether they enjoy work or their free time more, over sixty percent of the employed say they enjoy both equally or that they cannot choose between the two" (John P. Robinson, "Time for Work," *American Demographics,* April 1989, p. 68).

This finding was echoed in an article titled, "Detecting the Signs of Workaholic Behavior" in the *Wall Street Journal* (p. B-1, August 31, 1989). "With many managers routinely putting in sixty-hour work weeks, it may seem hard for them to know when they've crossed the line from simply working hard to the unhealthy obsession of workaholism," notes the article. "Once workaholism sets in, it progresses through stages similar to those of alcoholism and drug addiction. Among these: increased tolerance for more and more work, a feeling that 'you can't stop,' and anger and other withdrawal symptoms while away from work. Workaholics also tend to deny their addiction. You ask them if their round-the-clock schedules are a problem for them or their families and they insist 'everything's fine.' "

I recently saw early signs of workaholism exhibited during a once-in-a-lifetime adventure that I experienced over the Christmas holidays, 1989. My husband and I agreed to be leaders of a college youth group bound for a work camp in Belize, Central America. The location was remote, our accommodations were primitive, and our assigned work task—to put a roof on an orphanage—was difficult. Not only was our three-man, eight-woman work crew devoid of any roofing experience, but our missionary host had little in the way of tools and materials to offer us. The closest building supplier was a two-mile walk followed by a twenty-mile bus ride away.

The students had difficulty pacing themselves. Rather than designing six work days that sensibly balanced a variety of activities—so many hours of labor offset by mid-day rest periods and occasional outings to church, the city, and the beach—the students wanted to jump in and work nonstop until their task was done. They were frustrated when we had to call a halt to the project in order to trudge into town to gather nails and lumber. They were at loose ends when a heavy rain forced us indoors with nothing to do. Even in good weather they had trouble slowing down to the leisurely lifestyle of the natives. Particularly difficult was Sunday, which our host strictly observed as a day of rest.

"What will we do all day?" complained one young member of our workforce. "Let's get on with it," was the mood of the group. Even the most routine activities—going to church, preparing dinner, washing dishes—seemed pains-taking when we had to pump water for cold showers, rotate pots and pans on the two-burner stove to cook supper, and take turns washing and rinsing our utensils in small metal buckets. These campers were fast-track kids, after all, used to dashing from class to jobs to social events. They liked to attack every task with passion and push, push, push until it was done. They were over-achievers in training and they couldn't adjust to the forced leisure of a laid-back society. What's more, they didn't want to.

How about you? Why do you push? Would you be at odds with yourself if suddenly you had an abundance of leisure time? If Sunday truly was a day of rest? Which do you prefer, work or play? The answers to these questions should help you understand whether your life is in balance, and whether you can successfully separate who you are from what you do.

The encouraging truth is that many successful men and

women have proven that it *is* possible to be hard workers, high-achievers, and still to keep professional and personal identities apart and intact. Examples of people who maintain this delicate balance are everywhere. Take, for instance, General Colin L. Powell, the extraordinary man who was chosen by President George Bush to serve as chairman of the Joint Chiefs of Staff. Powell once told an interviewer that he had no secrets of success to share with the interviewer's audience. "Don't waste time looking for them," the general emphasized. "Success is the result of perfection, hard work, and learning from failure."

Perfection? Hard work? At first brush, Powell sounds like a workaholic, one who might have difficulty distinguishing who he is from what he does. And small wonder. Like all military people, he wears his success on his arms. And shoulders. And chest. Separating who he is from what he does is nearly impossible when what he does is so obvious in the stars, bars, medals, and clusters that decorate his uniform. Yet somehow he manages not to overidentify with his job. He works hard at this, and he claims as one of his personal guidelines this bit of advice: "Avoid having your ego so close to your position that when your position falls, your ego goes with it."

LEARN TO FAIL WELL

Remember that General Powell also credited *failure* with part of his success. Which brings up another question. How well do you fail?

One of the most serious pitfalls of overidentifying with a job is that it prevents us from taking chances. As Winston Churchill once said, "The maxim 'perfection' often spells paralysis." We become so overly concerned with performing to perfection that we fret about unimportant details and get bogged down in matters of little concern. We are afraid to break new ground and explore new ideas. To take a chance would be to risk failure, and to fail could cause a loss in self-esteem. Our self-worth might diminish in proportion to the size of the failures.

Christian counselors Dennis and Barbara Rainey of Little Rock, Arkansas, explain it this way: "Most women don't realize they can fail and not be failures. They haven't learned to separate their personal worth from their career performance. These women find it difficult to have their ideas, work, and goals criticized because they feel they, personally, are being criticized and rejected. If they can once get past that, life becomes far less of a burden to them."

Learning to fail well is such a valuable lesson that an industry is being created around it. The book *When Smart People Fail* refers to failure as the last taboo of our success-driven society and promises readers a plan to turn defeat into victory. The University of Michigan actually offers a course in failure, although it's not listed in any catalog that way. Officially, it's called "Innovative Entrepreneurship," but off the record and around campus it's known as "Failure 101." Class instructor Jack Matson has excellent credentials to teach the fine points of bellyupmanship: His Texas company went on the skids several years ago.

The course is no joke. Students strip failure of its stigma by looking at it from all angles. Matson and guest speakers openly discuss and dissect their down-the-tubes ventures, play out the what-if's in hindsights, and explore the how-to's of recovery. Students are then expected to experience failure firsthand by participating in doomed class business projects. Instead of junior achievement, this is senior setback. The result is that at the end of the semester, students have lost their fear of flopping and have gained an appreciation of risk-taking. They're ready for the real world and all of the slips, stumbles, and falls that await them there (*Wall Street Journal*, January 18, 1989, p. B-1).

If, up until now, men have been more successful than

women at career failure, it's only because they've had many more years to practice. As an example, take the Midwestern businessman of a century ago whose rèsumè documented an unbelievable string of defeats, collapses, and washouts. By the age of twenty-four, he had failed at business *twice* and already had lost a bid for the state legislature. During the next ten years he endured the death of his girlfriend, suffered a nervous breakdown, and was defeated in his campaign for Congress. More painful failures followed: Wedged between two losing attempts for the U.S. Senate was an unsuccessful run for the vice presidency.

Why didn't this incredible "loser" quit after a setback or two? It's simple. He was convinced he had a contribution to make in spite of all his defeats. He was able to fail without considering himself a failure. He took risks in the most public of all arenas—politics—and didn't give up until he was a winner, which he eventually was. His name: Abraham Lincoln.

What does all this mean to us? Simply this: As Christian women we can't allow ourselves to overidentify with our work and to become so immersed in *any* performance to the extent that if we fail, we consider ourselves failures. We can't always "play it safe" and never take risks. When we do that, we experience a more serious kind of failure. We have an obligation to God to explore, expand, and experiment with the gifts he has given us. How sad it would be to go through life oblivious to some special talents that are within us because we never took the time or took the chance to discover them.

No one knows this better than my friend Gloria Gaither, who, with her husband and partner Bill Gaither, left the security of high school teaching jobs twenty-five years ago for the risky business of writing and recording gospel music. Today a Grammy Award, a gold album, and several "Gospel Songwriter of the Year" citations decorate their wall of fame. They're at the top of their profession, and they're more determined than ever to take the same kind of risks as those they took to put themselves there. It often isn't easy, since risk-taking usually is linked to youth. Somehow it's all right to be "young and foolish" when you're trying to find your niche, but once you're forty and have "arrived," you're supposed to stay there. The problem with this? The only *sure* way to remain in one place is to tread water. This means repeating motions over and over without stretching beyond the familiar. The Gaithers refuse to do this.

"It seems everything we do at this stage has greater risk because it's so public," Gloria recently told me. "We used to be able to try out ideas and if they worked, fine. If they didn't, that was okay, too. We got where we are by risking, but in the early days the stakes weren't very high. Now it's not a 'quiet little failure' if we fail. To be perfectly honest, I think anybody who has created any kind of public attention is tempted to remain with the status quo and not do anything that would cause public failure. But if you succumb to that temptation, you're dead. I hope the Lord will always give us the courage to risk and risk big."

Gloria and Bill may have a long history of taking chances, but their success record is strong enough now to sustain a setback or two. But what about a risk-taker whose "happily-ever-after" ending hasn't been written yet? What about someone who left a lucrative career in gospel music to pursue a "quiet" career where success might be even more elusive? Let's meet such a person.

TAKING THE BIG RISK

Linda Mason has never been one to rest on her laurels. In the trendy terms of the day, she is a "handler." Or, at least she was until recently. The label "handler" surfaced during the 1988 Bush-Dukakis campaign and was used to describe the media/marketing experts behind the presidential candidates. George Bush's handler was James Baker; Michael Dukakis entrusted his handling duties to John Sasson. In their separate political camps Baker and Sasson created images, polished speeches, scheduled interviews, and supervised advertising campaigns.

Of course, Linda had nothing to do with presidential politics, and she'd probably cringe at the term "handler" because it smacks of manipulation. Somehow, pictures of either a horse trainer or a puppeteer come to mind. Linda is neither. In a very positive sense, for several years she worked as the expert in charge of boosting the public image of several of the world's most prominent Christian performers. Her duties varied from client to client, although many tasks were similar to those performed by presidential handlers on behalf of their candidates. For instance, she conducted a national promotion blitz for comedian Mike Warnke when Word Records released a new Warnke album; she created press publicity for Amy Grant; she designed media materials for Kellye Cash, Miss America of 1987; she developed Sandi Patti's first "awareness" campaign to introduce gospel music lovers to Sandi's gooseflesh-evoking high C range; and she managed the advertising and marketing efforts of several Bill Gaither Trio concert tours.

Although she has a sharp eye for opportunity, Linda never planned all of her personal success. And at the height of it, she never confused *who she was* with *what she did.* More importantly, she was confident enough to shed her highly visible, glamorous job and to take a gigantic risk when she felt God nudge her in a surprising new direction.

"I didn't consciously work at planning my life," she once told me. "I always had ideas of what I thought I wanted to do, but I never spent a lot of time in college making specific plans like students do today. After graduation, I taught for two years and got very involved in my church. I sensed that God wanted me in a ministry, but because of my sheltered background I thought of 'ministry' as my becoming the wife of a pastor. But I couldn't see myself in that role." She laughed. "I can't play the piano and I don't sing solos."

She was flexible, and when an offer to work at a school on Grand Cayman Island came her way, she grabbed it even though her father vehemently opposed the move. ("He thought I was going to some primitive place without indoor plumbing!") Her public relations talents surfaced as she planned the school's fortieth anniversary celebration and booked a benefit concert featuring a friend of a friend, Sandi Patti. Conversations with Sandi's husband/manager John Helvering eventually led to a job opportunity. Sandi's career was starting to soar and someone was needed to oversee the publicity efforts. Was Linda interested? She certainly was.

"I don't necessarily go out and try to make opportunities, but I recognize them when I see them," she said. "I started working for Sandi in 1982, and it seemed as if one thing just led to another. People in the gospel music industry became familiar with my reputation and a few of them called to ask if I'd like to work for them in Nashville. I said 'no' because it didn't feel right. I didn't want to build a big career. I've never had that kind of ambition for myself."

More important than the money was the challenge. Like so many of the women who completed my questionnaire, Linda values the feeling of satisfaction that comes from doing a job well. She has an excellent sense of what she can and can't accomplish. She likes to explore her God-given talents, and she isn't afraid to take risks to see how far those talents can take her. But she isn't driven. She's a high-achiever who isn't an over-achiever.

"My good points? I think that I'm very industrious and self-motivated. I initiate things pretty well, and I'm always trying to come up with ways to improve existing programs. I rarely stay stagnant, which probably is one reason I've moved from job to job every three or four years."

She also knows her shortcomings.

"If I don't feel that I'm in the place where God wants me to be, I don't do quite as well. I'm not as confident, not as motivated to push ahead."

As Sandi Patti's fame increased, so did Linda's responsibilities. Soon she was serving as liaison between Sandi and the media, the fans, and all sectors of the gospel music industry. She discovered talents she didn't know she had as she planned and taught publicity seminars for new and aspiring Christian artists. When she felt ready for a new challenge she considered several options and decided to join Bill Gaither's organization as director of public relations. There she developed, managed, and implemented publicity for a variety of performers. She expanded into market research and advertising. More "hidden" talents surfaced.

"Whatever job I've had, I've tried to treat it as a ministry," she said. "But I discovered along the way that my work wasn't completely satisfying even though I was helping to put forward the gospel, touch lives and, in many cases, change lives. The problem was that it wasn't firsthand experience for me. I was enabling someone else to have the experience. My contribution was indirect."

She wanted to make a change, but what kind of a change? She moved to Nashville, opened an agency, and quickly attracted several top Christian artists as clients. The work was "safe," familiar, yet still not satisfying. Something was missing. She prayed for direction. The nudge toward a ministry recurred. This time the possibilities included more than being a pastor's wife.

"I closed my agency and enrolled in a seminary class called 'Introduction to Ministry.' It helped me to evaluate the idea of me working in a church setting. After all those years I finally got a clear picture of where I should be. It wasn't a 'mystical call' into service, it was a quiet realization that the way I had lived my life clearly pointed me in this direction."

Reaction to her decision ranged from shock to applause. People who knew her professionally were surprised that she would walk away from a career that appeared to be so rewarding, so exciting. People who knew her personally cheered the move. "When I shared my decision with my long-term friends—people who have known me for fifteen and twenty years—they all said, 'Of course! This is so natural. This is who you are,'" recalled Linda.

But putting the plan into action required much more than the approval and blessings of friends. As a young, single woman, Linda still had to support herself while she attended seminary classes. She knew from experience that positions in promotions and marketing were too demanding to juggle with reading assignments and term papers. She needed steady work, a stable income, and lots of flexibility. She decided an office job would do nicely, thank you, and her ego had no problem with the idea of answering phones, typing memos, and filing documents. Such a position became available and she gratefully accepted it.

"And that's what has brought me to this place," she told me over lunch shortly after she started her new position. "For now, the farthest down the road that I can see is my goal of a seminary degree. It's a sixty-hour program and will lead to a master of religious education degree. It will take me a few years to complete it, but it's definitely what I want to do. I'm going to prepare myself, work full-time, attend school part-time, and be ready for whatever doors the Lord opens after that."

EXPLORE THE POSSIBILITIES

Linda Mason's experience teaches us two positive lessons. First, she didn't overidentify with her job to the point that her value became tangled in her title. Her self-esteem didn't diminish when she went from being Linda Mason, well-known publicist for gospel music stars, to being Linda Mason, seminary student and office worker. Second, although her work was very important to her, she was willing to take an enormous risk, leave the security of an established position, and experiment with a new way to serve God. Success in her field of publicity and marketing was a "sure thing"; success in the field of ministry is a question mark. It's possible that after years of study and sacrifice Linda may not find the right "doors" open to her after all. But she is willing to take the risk.

Whether a job ends by choice or by chance, we have two ways we can react to the situation. We can follow Naomi's model and become bitter and depressed until a new activity fills the void, or we can view change as a challenge and explore the possibilities that stretch before us. Paul reminded us:

> There are different kinds of service to God, but it is the same Lord we are serving. There are many ways in which God works in our lives, but it is the same God who does the work in and through all of us who are his.
>
> (1 Corinthians 12:5-7)

It's possible to serve God in different ways at different times in our lives. To do it, we have to be flexible like Linda Mason, be risk-takers like Bill and Gloria Gaither, and be willing to follow good advice from people like General Colin Powell. Remember his personal guideline: *"Avoid having your ego so close to your position that when your position falls, your ego goes with it."*

Positions do fall. Titles do change. Kids do grow up. Jobs are phased out. Retirement does happen.

But life goes on.

If we overidentify with our work, our self-esteem may be devalued when our work ends. If our job is our life, we may want to succeed at it so much that we play it safe and stay within the range of our experience, never daring to explore what else our God-given gifts might have enabled us to do.

Rather than helping us to accomplish more work, an addictive work ethic can *prevent* us from reaching our potential. It can blind us to opportunities, bind us to routine tasks, make us rigid, squelch our creativity, limit our contributions, and cause us to concentrate on the unimportant.

We've already seen this happen. In chapter two you met Judie, the young woman who let her parents, professors, and supervisors choose her work and decide her priorities. In chapter three you read about Sunny, the wife and mother who designed a ministry around her writing that was so rigid that it caused her to miss the opportunity to minister at home. As different as these women are, they share common traits. They had difficulty distinguishing between "who they were" and "what they did"; they feared failure; and they let their current occupation/preoccupation obscure their future opportunities.

Following Step 3 of the 12-Step Recovery Program could have spared Judie and Sunny much of their pain. Instead of turning over control of their lives to the "audiences" who applauded their performances, they could have relinquished it to God. The quality of their work wouldn't have changed, but their *attitude* toward their work would have been different. Like Gloria Gaither, Linda Mason, and others, they no longer would have feared defeat, they would have been willing to take risks, and, most importantly, they would have experienced the kind of wonderful serenity that comes with the knowledge that God is in control.

There *is* an alternative to over-achievement and workaholism. Now we know we can do more if only we will do less.

FIVE

Satisfaction Not Guaranteed

What a wonderful life I've had! I only wish I'd realized it sooner.

—Sidonie-Gabrielle Colette

I HAD FOUND THE PERFECT ILLUSTRATION, of all places, thrity-five thousand feet over Denver, enroute home from a West Coast writers' conference.

Like a lot of recovering workaholics, I subscribe to the Wilson Work Ethic which applies equally well to us women as to Kemmons Wilson, founder of the Holiday Inns chain. Wilson once said that a successful person has to work at least half a day, every day. "It doesn't matter *which* half he chooses to work," explained Wilson, "the first twelve hours or the last twelve."

As a champion of the Wilson work philosophy, I was using my time aloft to scratch out some notes for a public relations class lecture about the value of goal-setting. The purpose of the lesson was to show the students how long-term planning can keep an organization on track as it moves toward its desired destination. But I must have been at the end of my twelve-hour Wilson work shift because I wasn't feeling very creative, and the ideas weren't flowing. What I needed was a lively illustration to teach, not preach, the benefits of setting goals.

I found it in the USAir magazine, tucked in the seat pocket in front of me. It was an article about a study that had been conducted among Harvard University graduates several years out of school. Each of the alumni was asked whether or not he regularly set personal and professional goals. More than eighty percent of the grads said no, they set no formal goals for themselves; fourteen percent said yes, they identified goals but didn't write them down; and a scant three percent had committed their aspirations to paper.

Results? Using money as the yardstick to measure success, the grads who had set goals (but hadn't written them down) earned three times what their classmates without goals had earned. More phenomenal, the three percent who had written down their goals had made ten times as much as the non-goal-setting grads had made.

But here's the kicker to the story. Two days later, I entered the classroom prepared to enlighten my students on what goal-setting is all about and how it can be useful on a personal as well as a professional level. Because young people operate so much on a day-to-day basis and spend too much time in a knee-jerk mode *reacting* to problems rather than *acting* on their blueprint for the future, I was sure this lesson would be one of my more memorable.

"How many of you sit down on a regular basis and set personal and professional goals?" I challenged them. Nearly every hand shot up.

Hmmmmm.

"That's very good," I acknowledged, barely able to conceal my surprise. "But how many of you actually put your goals in writing and refer to them periodically?" Again, nearly every hand was raised. I was at a loss for words.

"How many of you read USAir's magazine?" I asked. The response shouldn't have surprised me. High-achieving people are avid list-makers and goal setters. Nearly everyone interviewed for this book admitted to some form of goal-setting, with the majority taking time to write their personal and professional objectives on paper and to scrutinize them weekly or monthly.

I'm no exception. My goals are carefully printed on index cards and are deposited in the small calendar that I always carry in my purse. These goals adhere to all the rules: They're specific, they're measurable, they include a deadline, and they're tough but attainable. For instance, last Christmas when I splurged and replaced my out-moded home computer with a state-of-the-art model, I knew that I probably would procrastinate in learning how to use it. I have always preferred the familiar to the unfamiliar, and there was *nothing* familiar about the strange little box with the tethered "mouse" that suddenly occupied the space next to Old Trusty, my vintage micro.

My mission was to master the alien being within two months. To make that happen, I set three short-term objectives. First, I pledged to make the transition from the dinosaur to the mystery machine by January 15; second, I committed myself to having the word-processing program fully mastered by the end of January; third, I planned to be producing sleek documents via the desk-top publishing option by mid-February. My obstacles to all this were easy to spot. There was my shortage of time to "play" at the keyboard, and there was my lack of interest in devouring the ho-hum owner's manuals—written in fluent computerese—that accompanied the new hardware. Somehow I would overcome these barriers to success. How did I do? Two out of three isn't bad—I have yet to "publish" a pie chart or a bar graph.

The whole purpose of goal-setting is to help us to focus on what we believe is important. It's a way of concentrating on the *results* we want to achieve rather than on the activities that keep us busy. Whenever torn between two ways to spend time, we can ask ourselves, "Which way will move me closer to achieving my goals?" The "right" choice quickly becomes evident.

It works. I remember first being introduced to the concept of goal-setting by radio commentator Paul Harvey several years ago. I was in Chicago to do a his-and-her profile of Harvey and his wife, Angel, who doubles as the producer of his popular broadcasts. I asked the couple if they had designed their dual career or if it had just happened. I'll never forget what Paul Harvey told me that afternoon.

"Angel seems dainty and ultimately feminine, but she has a will of iron," he said. "She really gives direction to our joint career because she's always known what she wanted us to do and be. When an opportunity comes along, all she has to do is ask, 'Is this on target? Or is it a detour? A shortcut? Or a digression?' When your guidelines are that simple, it's not difficult to stay on course. It's no wonder that in the case of Angel and me, one plus one equals eleven!"

As positive as goal-setting is, it can lose its value if taken to extremes. For a work-prone woman like myself, goals can be almost addictive. I have to guard against letting them occupy too much of my thoughts and attention. Like any addiction, there is a certain "high" attached to the "fix"—in this case, the tension of setting and the release of making the goal. Such a "high" is felt at the moment of accomplishment. Even if it's a personal goal that I've shared with no one, I celebrate its achievement and give myself inner strokes for having made it. Again, like so many addictions, the "high" is short-lived, and other goals quickly must be added to assure the continuation of the euphoric state.

The other danger of goal-setting is even more serious. Goal-setting can cause us to over-emphasize what *we* have decided is the correct course for our lives. *We* have put together this list of priorities and this blueprint for each day, week, and year, and *we* have focused all our attention and energy on accomplishing the plan.

But what about what God has in mind for us? What about his plan for us?

"DON'T TALK TO ME ABOUT CONTENTMENT"

One of the most driven women I have ever met does not work out of the home, has no aspiration to make a lot of money, and doesn't dream of someday building a career. Her name is Penny and she has cystic fibrosis, a fact that probably explains her fast-paced approach to life. At age thirty-six, she has already defied the odds. CF is considered to be a children's disease, with about half of its victims never reaching adulthood.

"I remember when I was in high school, I had such low self-esteem," she told me. "I felt like 'damaged goods' because there was so much wrong with my body. I was sick all the time; I was the smallest one in my class; I couldn't play in any sports, and no boys were ever attracted to me. I used to tell my mother that when God passed out talents I must have been in another room because I sure didn't get any. She always said my talent was that I survived. But that wasn't enough for me. My mother compared me with the other CF kids she knew from the support group. I compared myself with my classmates. By her measurement, survival was an accomplishment, by mine it was a 'given.'"

If you were to meet Penny, you'd think she is pretty in a fragile sort of way. Weight is an indicator of any CF victim's state of health, and Penny goes to great lengths to disguise her thinness under bulky sweaters in the winter and loose shirts in the summer. Still, when you ask her how she is, she generally responds in pounds. If her weight is up, she's fine, thank you; if her weight is down, she's discouraged. She's incredibly honest and impatient. She doesn't have time to be otherwise. Why? Because she's afraid she simply doesn't have time.

"I've dealt with limitations all my life," she said. "I've always been told that I can't do this or I can't do that because of CF. It's been almost like a challenge to me. I wanted to do well in school because everyone said that I couldn't. I wanted to go away to college because everyone said that I shouldn't. Most of all, I've wanted to be normal. I guess that's why I'm so driven. While most 'normal' people my age figure they have another thirty or forty years ahead of them, I'm not so sure. I have to cram more into my days and years because I may not have too many left. I have to work a little bit harder and a little bit faster than everyone else if I'm to get the same amount accomplished."

She's done much more than merely survive her thirty-six years. She's built an amazingly normal life in spite of her abnormal physical condition. An avid list-maker and goal-setter, she has been successful in achieving nearly everything she has set out to do. She is happily married (most CF victims don't marry), and she has two adopted children (many adoption agencies won't place children in homes where one of the parents has CF). If she has a problem, aside from the obvious, her illness, it's her lack of contentment. She's never at peace. She constantly sets goals for herself— seemingly impossible goals—and is restless and dissatisfied until she reaches them. Even after accomplishing her objectives she allows herself very little time to relax before she has scribbled a new set of aspirations on her agenda. Like an athlete who is always testing herself to see how far she can push herself, she chooses increasingly higher hurdles just to see if she can clear them.

"Don't talk to me about contentment," she said, laughing. "I'm not a contented person. When we were first married, I used to think, *if we could just adopt a baby I'd be satisfied.* And we were given Sarah. Before long, I was thinking, *if only we could adopt a second child, a little boy, I'd truly be content.* That's when we got Jaimie. Now I want a pregnancy of my own. I want my own biological baby, and then I'll be happy. I'm sure of it."

Many people close to her—myself included—wonder if a third baby is the answer. Or, is she still trying to prove to herself that she can do and can have what most of her friends around her can do and have? In other words, is she still trying to be "normal"? Recently she made the decision to home school her son, a tough undertaking for the heartiest mom. Even her husband, usually supportive, questioned the idea. But she credited the decision to God.

"The reason I'm doing it is because I believe God told me to do it," she said. "I'm sure I felt God's direction in this."

She also said she is certain that God wants her to have a third child, this one of her own flesh. Although her age and her health are against her, she is determined that she *will* become pregnant, and the pregnancy will bring her contentment.

But will this contentment be permanent? I asked.

"I don't know," she admitted.

And if God doesn't give her a baby—can she accept it? Pause.

"I don't know."

"I try to focus on the good things that have already happened," she said. "It helps ... but I wish it helped more."

PLAN TO FOLLOW HIS PLAN

St. Augustine once wrote, "Our hearts are restless 'til they find their rest in thee." I've often wondered if Penny's restlessness is caused by her concentration on *her* will rather than *his* will being done in her life. She focuses so intensely on *her* plans that she has convinced herself that they are *his* plans as well.

Penny's driving personality and her discontentment with

the status quo is not only harmful to herself, but it has a negative effect on her family. Her two young children sense that Mom is tense most of the time, and they wonder why she talks so much about having another baby. Why aren't they enough for her to love? Her husband knows he is powerless to fulfill his wife's needs and he is frustrated by this inability.

In the Twelve-Step Recovery Program for Over-Achievers three of the steps directly relate to the hurt that over-achievers cause their loved ones.

- I confess my mistakes to myself, to the people affected by my mistakes, and to God.

- I am aware of who has been hurt by my drivenness and I commit myself to finding ways to right those wrongs.

- I face the people I have hurt and make restitution.

Most driven persons, like Penny, are unaware that their push for perfection is harming anyone around them. They are so focused on what *they* want that they neglect the needs of others. It's not that they mean to be selfish, it's just that they're sure they know what is best. And they're determined to *make* it happen.

In a society motivated by slogans such as "if it's to be, it's up to me," many of us assume that we can control our destiny if only we focus hard enough on our chosen course of action. We have so much faith in our ability to plan our lives that we fail to trust God with any part of the plan. We dutifully write out our goals and then strike out in pursuit of them. Whenever we feel uncertain or tugged off course, we look down at our scribbles rather than up at our Lord for guidance and reassurance. But it's unlikely that we'll ever know real contentment until we say *and mean*, "thy will—not my will—be done." Even if we don't clearly see his goal for us, we have to trust that he has mapped our mission long before we ever read a self-help book or a how-to article that taught us the fine points of goal-setting. We must have faith that *he* knows the way even when *we* feel that we are lost.

One of my favorite illustrations of faith involves the life and ministry of Elisabeth Elliot, nationally known speaker and author of many books, including *Through Gates of Splendor*. I once collaborated on a book that included Mrs. Elliot's testimony, and I'll never forget how strongly she stressed the importance of accepting God's will. She said that she is often asked how she has coped with being a widow not once but twice in her life. Her first husband, missionary Jim Elliot, was murdered by a primitive tribe of South American Indians just twenty-seven months after their marriage. Her second husband, Addison Leitch, died of cancer. Years of widowhood followed both deaths. At one point in her solo life she lived in the jungle of South America and ministered to the same tribe that had killed her first husband. Why? Because she felt it was God's will, and to follow his will, not hers, has been her life's goal.

"During one of my periods of widowhood I was asked to talk to a group of seminary wives on the problems of being a widow," she recalled. "I refused. I said I'd be glad to talk to the seminary wives, but not on that topic. I didn't regard widowhood as a problem, but as the sphere in which I was to glorify God at that time. When I was single, I was to glorify God as a single; when married, I was to glorify God as a wife; when widowed, I was to glorify God as a widow.

"The best advice I can give anyone who is going through suffering of any kind is first to accept it, without gritting teeth, or clenching fists, or saying, 'Well, I guess I have to take this because it's the will of God,'" said Mrs. Elliot. "Too often people grudgingly say, 'This is my cross to bear.' Instead, why not say, *Yes, Lord, gladly I will accept this for your sake*" (*First Person Singular*, by Jerry Jones and Holly Miller, Impact Books, pp. 100-101, 1981).

How well this relates to Steps eleven and twelve of the Twelve-Step Recovery Program!

- As I work to strengthen my relationship with God I ask only to know his will for me.

- My goal is to live my life according to God's plan and thereby to serve as an example for others.

One of the challenges we all face is maintaining our focus after we've charted our course. Sometimes, in making this point to students, I tell them about long-distance swimmer Florence Chadwick, best known for her successful swims, in both directions, across the English Channel. But this illustration took place later, after her victory over the channel, when her goal was the twenty-one-mile stretch of icy water between Catalina Island and the coast of California. The feat had never been accomplished by a woman, and Florence, at age thirty-four, was determined to be the first to claim the honor.

Talk about pressure! The chosen date for the swim was July 4, 1952, a holiday, and much of the country was watching on television. The drama was heightened by commentators who described in colorful hyperbole the heavy fog, the cold water, and the persistent sharks. At several points during the swim, rifles had to be blasted over the waves to fend off the hungry sharks. Undaunted, Florence kept stroking hour after hour as she moved closer and closer to her goal. But victory wasn't to be hers that day. Surprisingly, what finally ended her bid for success wasn't fatigue or fear, but fog and her lack of faith.

After nearly sixteen hours in the water, she complained of numbness. She squinted to see the shore, but the soup-like fog reduced her visibility to almost zero. After so much time, she reasoned, she should have been able to see her destination—her goal. Instead, more fog. More cold, turbulent waves. She called to her mother and her trainer in the rescue boat. She couldn't go on, she shouted. She wanted to be pulled to the warmth and safety of the craft. They encouraged her to continue, but when she looked toward where her goal should have been, again she saw nothing. She begged them to end her misery.

Florence was finally pulled from the water, shivering and defeated. Imagine her dismay when she learned that she was only half a mile from her destination. She knew that physically she could have done it; her body had been conditioned for the distance, but mentally she hadn't been trained for the uncertainty. Later, she told reporters that she wasn't making excuses for her failure, but "if only I could have seen land, I know I could have made it."

She was right, she *could have* made it. Just a few weeks later she attempted the same swim, under the same foggy conditions, and she finished the course in record time. Not only did she become the first woman to complete the icy stretch, but she beat the men's record by two hours! The difference the second time, of course, was that she had faith in spite of her inability to see. She had the same kind of faith that is "the substance of things hoped for, the evidence of things not seen" (Hebrews 11:1).

IN PURSUIT OF BALANCE

The stories of Penny, Elisabeth Elliot, and of Florence Chadwick make two important points, both relating to balance. In Penny's case, she failed to accept the idea that her goals may not be in harmony with God's goals for her. She was so certain that what she aspired to was right, that she transferred her aspirations onto God and claimed them as his aspirations. She was like the elderly novice writer whom I once encountered at a writers' conference. The woman thrust a typewritten manuscript at me (I was at the workshop as *The Saturday Evening Post's* representative) and explained, "God told me that *The Post* would want to publish this." One quick read-through assured me that the story was totally inappropriate for the magazine, and it was the writer, not God, who was convinced of its placement in *The Post*. Of course, trying to explain my decision to the writer was a major task. In her eyes, I was going against God's will.

Balance. Somehow we have to curb our own enthusiastic goals and stop pushing for their accomplishment long enough to be aware of God's goals. As Elisabeth Elliot urges, we should say, *Yes, Lord, gladly I will accept this for your sake.* What we want and what he wants should be one and the same.

Florence Chadwick, on the other hand, is an example of one who gave up the pursuit of her goal when she lost sight of it. Again, balance needs to be the key. We have to be quietly assured that the course we have set for ourself with God's guidance is the right course. We shouldn't waver from that course even when we can't see where it is leading. Our goals, once set, will be met if we have faith.

The perfection-prone woman periodically has to check her goals, not only to make sure she's moving toward their accomplishment, but to make sure they are God's goals as well as her own, that she is dedicated to them even when they seem elusive, and that they haven't become addictive to the point that they are crowding out other important aspects of her life.

A teacher friend of mine, Connie, jokes that her husband used to scribble additions to her many goal lists. He would write items such as "watch football game on TV with spouse" and "sleep late (at least 7 A.M.) on Saturday." Obviously, her adherence to these lists had been a source of friction as well as jokes throughout their twenty-year marriage.

"I don't set many long-range goals," Connie told me. "It's a weekly thing with me. Every Sunday night I sit down and make a list of what I have to do after work each day. I keep another list of what has to be done at the office. I always accomplish these daily goals. I couldn't go to bed at night if I didn't. For instance, on Tuesday evenings I always do the books for my husband's medical office. I remember one Tuesday night when I had a meeting and I didn't get home until after midnight. Jack, my husband, had left a note on the desk saying not to worry, that the books could wait a day. But I couldn't do that. I stayed up until I finished the job."

Connie admitted that she fights her non-stop work compulsion every day of her life. At age forty-five, she has workaholism under control most of the time and under surveillance all of the time. Over the years she has learned to turn off her teaching job once she leaves the classroom, but then she goes home and turns on her housekeeping duties in an equally compulsive way. She depends on feedback from family and coworkers to let her know when she has gone too far and is losing her balance.

"A frequent complaint about me at work is that I'm inflexible," she said.. "It kind of hurts my feelings, but so many people have said it that it has to be true. I know I need to ease up; if a job doesn't get done exactly on schedule the world isn't going to end, I tell myself. If Wednesday's goal isn't achieved until Thursday afternoon, who cares?

"I've also been accused of being a micromanager. I give people jobs to do and then I constantly check up on them. A lot gets done under my supervision but people don't like it. It reached the point a couple of years ago that three people on my teaching team would hardly speak to me. I went to my supervisor and said, 'What am I doing wrong?' He laughed because he had been watching and knew exactly what I was doing, but he wanted me to discover it on my own. So, I've made a conscious effort to back off; I still have to make certain assignments, but then I let the people carry out the assignments in their own way. It's hard for me—I always want to be asking 'How are you doing?'—but I force myself to let go."

Like work itself, goal-setting is a positive activity. It gets things done on time. Entire businesses today are run by a philosophy called management by objectives (MBO) which has company employees—from the CEO to the production workers—setting long-term and short-term goals for themselves and their organizations. The idea is to focus on a destination, decide on a route, and then travel that route without detour or delay. It's a trendy concept that has been the topic of books, the subject of college courses, and the purpose behind many employee training programs.

But focusing on what a person or an organization wants to accomplish and pulling out all the stops to achieve it is nothing new. As the Apostle Paul wrote to the Corinthians:

> To win the contest you must deny yourselves many things that would keep you from doing your best. An athlete goes to all this trouble just to win a blue ribbon or a silver cup, but we do it for a heavenly reward that never disappears. So I run straight to the goal with purpose in every step. I fight to win. I'm not just shadow-boxing or playing around. Like an athlete I punish my body, treating it roughly, training it to do what it should, not what it wants to. Otherwise I fear that after enlisting others for the race, I myself might be declared unfit and ordered to stand aside. (1 Corinthians 9:25-27)

Paul wasn't talking about breaking a swim record such as Florence Chadwick did, or overcoming the obstacles of a dreaded disease such as Penny did, or turning in a first-class performance as a teacher-homemaker such as Connie did. He was referring to a higher objective, the kind of goal that supersedes all others. He was talking about the sort of life goal that Elisabeth Elliot set for herself as a young woman and has followed ever since.

The most important objective that each of us has to accomplish in her lifetime is to learn God's will for us, accept it, make it our will as well, and then to pursue it relentlessly. Whether goals are set daily, weekly, or annually, deciding on a second goal is the most difficult. The first is easy: *Thy will be done.*

SIX

Intimacies

Do OVER-ACHIEVING WOMEN MAKE GREAT FRIENDS AND LOVERS? Most of the men I surveyed said, "Well yes, Dennis, but only when they have the time."

Quite often the husband of an over-achieving female will claim that his wife was transformed from an enthusiastic, passionate lover to a regulated, functional sex partner as her activities demanded more and more of her time. One man claimed that he even saw "sex with Bob" penciled on his wife's monthly planning calendar at four-day intervals, as though he were a mandatory obligation of his wife's rather than a spontaneous enjoyment for her.

Whereas the intimacy factor is usually centered on sexual satisfaction, or the lack of it, a much more basic question is whether or not over-achieving women simply lose *all* basic elements of intimacy. Many would say the answer is yes.

Consider Carly B., a successful thirty-four-year-old attorney. Carly has been married to Ron, a civil engineer, for nine years. Their combined incomes exceed $100,000 annually. They own a beautiful home, drive new cars, and are members of the country club. Carly and Ron have no children and probably never will have any, by choice. They both love their careers and they each work about sixty hours per week. Carly is attractive, smartly dressed at all times, and quick-witted. Her only problem in life is that she has no friends. She has many acquaintances, but *no friends*.

She finds weekends boring and she can't wait for Monday to come around so that she can go back to her law firm. At the office there are people she can relate to and plenty of activities to keep her occupied.

If you were to ask her about her circle of friends, as I did, she might show you her jam-packed calendar. But while she may *think* she has close friends, time proves her wrong about that. She may consider her secretary to be a friend; yet, when her secretary marries and stops working to start a family, she seldom, if ever, keeps in contact with Carly. Likewise, there are clients Carly has serviced for many years and whom she calls by their first names. She considers them her friends; yet, in truth, not one of them would be the sort of person she would tell her personal secrets to or call up and invite out for lunch and a movie.

At times Carly will catch herself daydreaming about her years of living in a dormitory while in college. Those were zany times. She and her roommates, Doris and Belinda, used to share a pizza at midnight, swap each other's wardrobes in a free-for-all of mix and match, stay awake all night talking about boys, and visit each other's homes during semester breaks. They fixed each other's hair, traded notes from chemistry class, and worked together on the homecoming float. It was all such fun. There were so many laughs and secrets and surprises and plans. If ever three girls were meant to be lifetime friends, surely these three were.

But what happened? How is it possible that ten years slipped by and no contact has been made except for the perfunctory sending of an annual Christmas card (printed with "Happy Holidays from Mark and Doris," with no note enclosed)? Did priorities change that drastically?

Yes, priorities did change: for Carly, the most important thing became earning top grades at law school; for Doris, the most important thing became getting married and landing her first job as an elementary school teacher; for Belinda, the most important thing became leaving America and doing two years of graduate art studies in Paris and Madrid.

Besides priorities, however, horizons changed. As a corporate lawyer, Carly identified with big cities, swank office buildings, and the trappings of tangible success. As a teacher, Doris liked the dependability of a nine-month job in the same school building in the same small town year after year. As an artist, Belinda saw the world as her home and, as such, she was just as content to accept a grant to study sculpture for a year in Greece as she was to serve as a guest lecturer in humanities for a summer in Hawaii.

The major difference in the three women, however, was not their choice of careers, but their choice of relationships. Doris lived in a neighborhood where her kids played with the other kids, and all the moms knew each other, and there were church socials and school functions to attend, and everybody helped everybody else in the traditional small town way. With summers off, Doris developed an interest in crafts and other hobbies. She was a member of a weekly bridge club, a Bible study group, and the teachers' association. She had many friends and a very full life.

Belinda traveled a lot, but she used Paris as a base. She kept a small apartment in the artists' community. Her neighbors were all struggling artists, and they survived by scrounging from whoever among them had made a sale of some kind that week. Belinda never ate alone. If Maria, the chalk artist, earned a commission, she would throw a party and invite everyone in. If Pierre, the muralist, was still broke, he would knock at Belinda's door and invite himself for lunch. Belinda loved these people and loved this life, and everyone loved her, too. It was camaraderie at its best.

Carly, however, had none of the friendship bonds that Doris and Belinda had. Carly had her work and her husband. And since her husband was a workaholic, Carly didn't even have him as often as she might have liked. So, she relied on work to fill the gaps of intimacy she felt in her life. Work didn't reward her amply, however, and at times she would lie awake in bed at night and feel lonely. This would scare her because she knew of no way to solve this problem. She had skills and money and prestige, but she didn't have even one honest-to-goodness friend.

DEVELOPING TIES THAT BIND

In Ecclesiastes, Solomon warned, "Woe to him that is alone when he falleth; for he hath not another to help him up" (Ecclesiastes 4:10). Substitute "she" for "he" and many over-achieving women feel that this verse is directed straight at them. It's a fact: Over-achieving men *and* women often don't make friends easily. They choose not to. "Too busy," they say. "Not enough time."

Good friends not only "help us up" when we fall, but they often prevent us from stumbling in the first place. They do this by letting us know when we're losing our balance. They listen to us, help us to sort through our problems, distract us, amuse us, make us laugh at ourselves, and pull us into their lives so we don't become overly concerned with ours.

If you've resolved to slow down, ease up, and strike a better balance in your life, one way to do it is to develop and nurture meaningful friendships. How do you begin? These twelve steps can help.

TWELVE STEPS TO BETTER RELATIONSHIPS

1. Develop different kinds of friendships. If you were to look up "friend" in a thesaurus, you'd find at least a dozen words that have *almost* but not quite the same meaning— colleague, associate, buddy, confidant, playmate, travel companion, bedfellow, sidekick, listening post, chum, crony, schoolmate, compatriot. They're similar, but not identical. And there's a lesson to be learned in that.

We all need a variety of friends. One friend may serve as a mentor, another may be our jogging pal, a third may be someone who shares our fascination with historical novels, a fourth may be someone for whom *we're* acting as a mentor, a fifth may be our prayer partner. Not all friends fill all roles. That's why we need to cultivate diverse relationships.

2. Seek friends in different age groups. Some of the greatest friendships in history—Paul's and Timothy's, for instance—have existed between people of different ages. Young friends keep us alert and give us new perspectives; older friends offer us wisdom and experience. What a shame that our society endorses apartment complexes for singles only, surburban developments for couples with young children, and retirement condos for the sixty-plus set. Whatever happened to the multi-generational community?

3. Seek friends of both sexes. Communication between the sexes has cut down on the old competitiveness and given rise to a new camaraderie. Men and women often look at problems from different bases of experience. By sharing opinions they can achieve a better balanced picture.

4. Cultivate short-term and long-term friendships. Not all friendships are meant to last a lifetime. I remember two women who were the driving forces behind forming a high school band boosters organization in my hometown. This twosome worked tirelessly to organize fundraisers, rally support among parents, and chaperone a trip to the Macy's Parade in New York. They were on the phone to each other frequently, sewed uniforms side by side, and often shared seats on the bus when the band competed in out-of-town marching contests.

The irony of their friendship was that after their sons had graduated from high school and their involvement with the band ceased, they found they had little in common. They still liked each other very much, but without the activity that had bonded them, they had little to talk about beyond "the old days."

It's important for us to know that some friendships may flourish for a few months or for a few years and then, for a variety of reasons, may diminish in intensity. And that's all right.

5. Cultivate and nurture long-term friendships. While many relationships come and go, some are special and deserve to endure for a lifetime. Friendships—even the best ones—are fragile and have to be nurtured carefully. For instance, I know of two former sorority sisters who now live on opposite coasts. They were practically inseparable during their college years, but now see each other only once every three or four years. Still, on the first Sunday afternoon of the month they spend about an hour on the phone catching up on news of husbands, kids, and jobs. They anticipate those long-distant visits with just as much excitement as if they were going to sit down face-to-face.

6. Learn to break down barriers. Let's be honest. Today's society simply isn't conducive to friendships. Visible barriers include privacy hedges, fences, security gates, and mini-blinds. Invisible barriers are busy schedules, overtime hours, and jobs that have us changing locations every three to five years. Friendships aren't likely to sprout over backyard fences these days. We have to work at making them work.

7. Avoid suffocating friendships. Not all friendships are good for our health. Sometimes a friend will want to dominate our time. When phone calls are too frequent and too long, and when lunch dates become burdens rather than treats, it may be time to call a halt to the togetherness. I have known of friends who become too possessive and resent their friends having other relationships. Those are the friendships that *cause* rather than *curb* stress.

8. Don't be "too good" a friend. While it's always good to listen to a friend's problems and help her shoulder her burden, it isn't good to assume her problems as your own. Sometimes a friend can "unload" her troubles onto you and feel much better for doing it. You, however, are left depressed under the weight of it all! Guard yourself from feeling over-responsible for helping another who is struggling. Don't allow yourself to become a dumping ground for her. Keep the relationship healthy.

9. Don't be a fair-weather friend. Real friends are available during bad times as well as good. You may be in the mood for laughter and fun, but she may require counsel and support. Be willing to tune into a friend's needs and do your best to fill them.

10. Share victories as well as defeats. Sometimes it's easier on our ego to weep with a friend rather than to celebrate with her. Competitive over-achievers may find it difficult to applaud a friend who has reached greater heights than the over-achievers have reached. Don't allow jealousy and personal discontent to sour a friendship. When women compare themselves with one another, true bonds of friendship become very difficult to build.

11. Don't collect friends like trophies. Too many superficial friendships can wear you out. Sometimes we feel we have to "perform" for people we don't know very well. We have to be upbeat, and never let down our guard. Good friendships should have a refreshing, replenishing effect. If our circle becomes too wide, we may exhaust ourselves making the circuit.

12. Build friendship time into your schedule. Look at your calendar and identify regular times that you can set aside to develop and nurture friendships. Sometimes this takes real creativity. I recall when I was in graduate school and working two part-time jobs, it was all I could do to spend a couple of precious hours each day with my wife and young son. Still, we knew we both needed the company of good friends to take some of the drudgery out of our grueling schedule. With a little planning, we set aside two hours after church each week and got into the delightful habit of inviting friends in for Sunday brunch. It was inexpensive—we were on a tight budget—and it rejuvenated us for another week of books and work.

CONFRONTING THE LONELINESS

Carly, and thousands like her, could benefit from these twelve steps. These women are over-achievers who have trophies, awards, money, opportunities to travel, fancy offices, limousines—everything except intimate relationships. On the outside they appear "together," but on the inside many are empty.

Some women have learned ways to form friendships. They've learned the value of putting their husbands and other family members and friends high on their list of priority concerns. A few could not see their situations for what they were, but thanks to patient and helpful spouses or friends these women saw the need to change their lifestyles.

Consider the case of Amy and Charles. While in college this twosome fell in love. They were married when Amy was twenty-three and Charles was twenty-two. They both landed jobs as high school teachers in the same building. They bought a comfortable little home and after five years they started a family. After giving birth to twins, she took a four-year leave of absence to spend time with their babies. On Saturdays and two nights each week, however, she attended graduate school to study school administration. When her twins began pre-school at age four, Amy hired a part-time housekeeper and babysitter. She then returned to work full-time, but now as principal of a middle school.

Amy had missed having an outside job. She thrived in her new position. She arrived at work at 6:30 A.M. and never came home until after 5:00 each night. She held teacher meetings, directed faculty training, visited the classrooms as an observer, reorganized the school library, developed a computer lab for seventh graders and met one-on-one with parents of students who needed special attention. On two occasions she was written about in the local newspapers. Other school districts invited her to lead in-service seminars for them on student motivation.

Charles was patient the first year Amy returned to work. Although he missed their time together, he felt it was his role to encourage her while she adjusted to her new position. Unfortunately, Amy's success compounded itself to the point that she had almost every night planned for a meeting or seminar or lecture. This continued year after year. Charles became more vocal about his need for personal time with Amy, but she always put him off with, "Just as soon as this project is done." But there was always another pressing project to take its place.

Then one day Charles tried a different tack. When Amy came home at 5:00 that night, Charles gave her a purse-sized bottle of Georgio and a rose. He told her he had sent the housekeeper home early and that he had driven the twins across town to spend the night with Amy's mother. Charles then took Amy out to dinner and still had time to drive her back to her school building by 7:30 P.M. when a PTA meeting began. Later, Charles picked her up at 10:00 and drove her home. They went right to bed and made love.

For the next several days Amy was right back into her

rigorous routine of early mornings, late nights. On Saturday she was straightening their bedroom in the morning. The rose Charles had given her was in a vase on her dresser. It now was drooping and wilted, so she threw it in the wastebasket. Later that day Charles retrieved it and put it back in the vase. Amy saw it and asked him what he was doing.

"That's a marriage barometer," Charles explained. "For the next year each time we spend some private time together and end up making love, I'm going to buy a new rose for the vase. If the rose in the vase is dying and losing its beauty, then our marriage will be in the same condition. If the rose is open and fresh, then our marriage will be that way, too."

Amy looked at the dry, wilted rose with its lost petals. She smiled. "Today would be a good day to go buy a new rose, don't you think?" she asked.

AVOIDING SPOUSE ALIENATION

Fortunately, Charles was able to make his "statement" with a rose. Amy was an over-achiever, all right, but not to the point of missing Charles's point. Sometimes the "fix" isn't that easy.

Dr. Paul Meier, Los Angeles-based psychiatrist and partner in the nationally known Minirth-Meier Clinics, says that many people focus on achievement in order to avoid focusing on feelings. Perhaps these people have been rejected or neglected in some earlier relationships—either by their parents, their siblings or others—and are afraid of being rejected again. Perhaps they feel insecure and believe they are failures at intimate relationships. After all, Mom and Dad had known them better than anyone and yet Mom and Dad had rejected them. And so the barriers go up. The over-achievers decide if they keep themselves busy enough, they won't have time to develop deep relationships. Work prevents people from getting close and being in a position to hurt the over-achiever. Also, the applause that the "performer" reaps from turning in her dazzling performance soothes those old wounds that were caused by rejection.

Depending on how serious the wounds are and what caused them in the first place, professional help may be needed. Here's a good way to know if your drive is healthy or unhealthy, and if you can slow your pace yourself or if you need outside counseling. Try some of the ideas listed below. They are suggestions that have been shared with us by couples who have battled over-achievement/perfectionism in their marriages. They are simple, pragmatic action plans that *could* make a difference in your life. If they are too difficult for you to initiate, you may need the help of a qualified psychologist or family counselor.

The 80/20 Vacation Plan. By nature, over-achievers loathe vacations. The very mention of sharing a lonely mountain lodge with friends for a week of chess and nature hikes is enough to cause an over-achiever to experience cabin fever. Over-achievers need work the way amphibians need water: they can't stay away from it for too long a time.

Still, we all (yes, even over-achievers) need vacations and rest periods. The solution one wife and her husband developed involves an eighty percent pleasure and twenty percent work vacation. When she and her husband fly out of state for a week of fun, he says nothing when she puts in two hours of work in the morning (doing some writing or appearing on a TV talk show or giving a lecture at a conference or convention). After that, they spend the rest of the day together sunbathing, shopping, or sight-seeing.

Many times the couple will take their two children and just reverse the day's order. They will have their family fun together until 3 P.M. and then the wife will put in a couple of hours of work alone while the husband and kids visit a museum or swim in the motel pool. Rather than *criticize* his wife for not "letting go" completely while on vacation, the husband *thanks* her for allowing him and the children to be able to go on so many nice trips each year.

If you feel uneasy during vacations, you could use the same 80/20 system. Each morning you could make a call to your office or to some special clients. You could spend time reading some new product brochures or textbooks or you could work on some of your long-range projects. After two hours of work, your work-related conscience would be at ease and your readiness for fun would be at a peak.

Encourage Independent Pursuits. Being married to an over-achiever does not mean a spouse has to give up his or her own interests. In fact, the opposite should occur. The spouse should develop new hobbies, begin to join new organizations, and pursue interests of his or her own choosing.

One woman we surveyed was a professional consultant who was often away from home. Even when she *was* home, she required a lot of privacy so that she could work with her personal computer. Her husband compensated for this by pursuing some independent interests. He plays the banjo, plants his own garden, and spends a lot of time reading. He has a regular forty-hour per week job working in a music store, but he also sings in a men's quartet at church, plays in the city orchestra, and occasionally writes music reviews for the local newspaper.

Needless to say, this husband and wife never lack for anything to discuss. They are both active and involved in separate careers while also maintaining a mutual devotion to each other, their church, and their friends. So, if you are a high-achiever, encourage your spouse to be more than just a sideline observer. Suggest some ideas for independent interests which he can develop.

Provide Access to Finances. One of the most common reasons an over-achieving career woman will give for working fifteen-hour days is not the truthful one—"Oh, how I love this job!"—but rather some version of, "We really need the extra money." That was the excuse one woman said she used for several years as she squirreled away her earnings. Then one day her husband shocked her with the news that he was going to buy a boat. The wife immediately protested that they couldn't afford it.

"Look," said the husband, "you're logging all kinds of hours Monday through Saturday. If we can't afford some nice things now, we never will. So, what's it going to be?"

The next day they bought the boat. After that they bought a new compact disc player and a new living room suite. The wife realized the husband was right. Anyone willing to live with an over-achiever's crazy hours and schedules and habits deserves some of the benefits from the over-achiever's efforts. Fair is fair.

Engage in Frank Discussions. Over-achieving women are often single-minded, determined, and purposeful—but that doesn't always mean they are right. One respondent to our survey wrote, "I fall short of the mark many times. Fortunately, my husband has enough sincere concern to point out (in a loving but direct way) some of the areas I need to improve in. By being respectful of what he says, I've been able to learn a lot and to avoid potential problem areas."

She continued, "My husband and I engage in a lot of frank discussions. We see nothing productive in sulking, ignoring each other, or displaying pig-headed obstinance. As such, we try to 'clear the air' whenever something nags at us."

Another woman wrote, "I'm not saying it's a joyful event when my husband tells me I need to lose ten pounds or that I'm spending too much time teaching my seven-year-old daughter to cross-stitch and not enough time reading to her. Still, that's the best way to handle a workaholic like me.

Bluntness is best. Because my mind is always racing, subtleties are not effective. Besides, bluntness gets to the point right away and saves time. Workaholics love to save time."

So, take an hour or two one night and get your spouse to really talk to you. If it turns out that in your hustle and bustle you've forgotten to give a card on an anniversary or your constant use of the car has become a selfish habit or you've allowed your social life as a couple to dry up, apologize (*sincerely*) and then start to make amends. Keep those conversation channels open and don't let your ego make you blind to your faults.

Use Time-Saving Devices. Workaholics usually try to put people on their schedule rather than adapt to other people's schedules. That's not so easy to do with a spouse who has children to care for or a full-time job of his own to contend with. One of the ways to get around this, however, is to use machines to "buy time" for you and your spouse.

If you want to talk to your husband after dinner, you might want to consider investing in an automatic dishwasher. If you want to talk to your husband on Friday nights, but he needs to wash and wax the car, you could save him the time by taking the car to a drive-through car wash on Fridays. The same work will be accomplished as always, but it will be done by machines so you can use the time saved to talk with your spouse.

Delegate Authority Roles. Many workaholics become workaholics by assuming they have to do *everything* in order for it to be done right. That sort of attitude can be extremely offensive to a spouse. Instead, the workaholic should show enough respect for the spouse to allow him to handle major responsibilities, too.

One respondent told us, "During the first five years of our

marriage, I handled all of our finances, from the bill paying to the savings depositing. Later, I was holding two part-time jobs while finishing my Ed.D. in secondary education. Something had to give. I turned over all the budgeting and all the financial responsibilities to my husband. He met the challenge so well, he's been in charge of our family finances ever since. He has gained such confidence in this area of financial management over the years, he's now also doing our annual state and federal tax returns, as well as negotiating bank loans we need, pledging our tithes to our home church, and helping our children with their Christmas clubs. It's great!"

Ask for Career-Related Assistance. You know that old line that goes, "If you can't beat 'em, join 'em." If you are an over-achiever, you should reverse that adage and make it, "If you can't change me, then join me."

One woman told us, "If I'm rushed to meet a deadline, my husband will often help me with my typing chores. If I need a second opinion on something I've written, my husband will read it and offer revision suggestions. If I'm short on time in completing a research project, my husband will go to the library to get books for me. This not only helps him keep aware of the projects I'm working on, but it also provides a way for us to work and be together."

You can do the same thing. If you have to attend a conference, maybe your spouse will go along to help with the driving duties and then help you set up your display table. If your phone logs, appointment books, and expense records need to be reorganized, your spouse may be willing to do the job.

Rather than having the idea that you are boring your spouse with "shop talk" or "dull business routines" when you ask him for help, think instead of the chances you'll have to spend time together. Your spouse may not wish to get involved in your work, but you won't know until you ask.

Appreciate Psychic Income. It's true over-achievers deprive their spouses and families of much of their time. And they are frequently criticized by their spouses for it. What should be remembered, however, is that all efficient over-achievers also provide many spin-off benefits for their family members which other people are not privileged to. It's not wrong to remind your spouse of such benefits.

One of our survey respondents wrote, "My husband wishes that I weren't so work-oriented all the time. Nevertheless, he's honest enough and open enough to admit that he gets 'a kick' out of being able to go along on company trips to Bermuda with me, and it's an inner thrill for him each time he's in the crowd when I stand up to give a speech."

Use Tandem Scheduling. Coordinating calendars was a suggestion that came in from both the women *and men* who responded to our surveys. Several said that by knowing well in advance what their individual and family plans were, they were able to accomplish things simultaneously.

"I needed to do a lot of Christmas shopping," wrote one woman, "and when I looked at the calendar I saw that my husband Mike had a convention booking in Cincinnati the first week of December. So, I postponed my shopping until then. I went to Cincinnati that week with Mike. He spent every morning in workshops and I spent every morning shopping. At noon we would have lunch together and then we'd spend the afternoons swimming in the hotel pool, taking in a movie, or touring the convention's display booths. By coordinating our schedules we both got our work done, yet still had time to be together."

Another woman wrote, "I used to work as assistant

manager in a florist's shop. My husband is an hourly worker at a manufacturing plant. Whenever he would be put on second shift, we would never see each other. Ted had no control over his shift changes, but I missed seeing Ted. To resolve this, I obtained a real estate license and quit my job at the florist's. Now, when Ted is on the day shift, I sell real estate during the days; when he's on the night shift, I show homes during the evening. We both get to work, yet we also have time to be with one another."

Some respondents noted that there are certain days on the family calendar which are never to be violated, such as *everyone* attends church together on Sunday and Wednesday nights; or Saturday morning is *always* family work time around the house; or Monday evening is family activity night at home. This guarantees that there will be an anchor to family life that will keep individual family members from drifting off in all directions.

Give In—On Both Sides. My mother used to tell me that marriage harmony was a sixty-forty proposition: each spouse had to give in sixty percent of the time and hold the line forty percent of the time. Years ago, when I first heard that, I thought it was cute. Today, after nearly twenty years of marriage, I wonder why those words aren't in the Bible or the encyclopedia or some other respected book—they really are true!

Both the spouse and the over-achiever need to develop tolerance, respect, indulgence, and appreciation for the other person. Before they criticize each other's habits or behavior, they should attempt to understand the reasons behind such developments. Think about compromise rather than criticism. Think about alternatives rather than arguments. Think about family dètente rather than family debate. Success at your work is of no value to you if you fail on the home front. It's no crime to be a diligent worker—just know what you're working for and why.

OVERVIEW

We have seen in this chapter that one of the most serious problems over-achieving women often confront is having a lack of intimate relationships, both on the level of friendships and on the level of marital unity. This can put these women into an emotional desert, where there is no fellowship or bonding with people even of the same age groups, same sex, same neighborhoods, or same socio-economic levels.

Fortunately, we noted that there are ways to correct this situation. Sometimes, an understanding spouse or a friend needs to give the over-achieving woman an object lesson (a dying rose) or a serious talk in order to turn her back to intimate relationships she may be in danger of jeopardizing. Other times, the over-achiever needs to take steps herself to initiate or rekindle fading relationships. We discovered seven specific things that could be done to achieve this.

Finally, we noted that even when marital intimacy is established, it needs to be nurtured and protected in a variety of ways. We heard from several women about the methods they and their husbands have used to prevent spouse alienation.

If you've felt lonely or alienated at times, read this chapter again and take careful note of the steps you can take to re-establish strong relationships in your life. There's no need to walk through life alone.

SEVEN

Part-Time/Short-Term Over-Achievers

MY SISTER PAM HENSLEY has "spurted" her way up the ladder of success. Some career women focus on a specific goal they want to achieve in life and they steadily inch their way toward it over a period of years. Other women focus on a goal and approach it with alternating phases of bursts of blinding speed and times out for rest and reassessment. My sister definitely falls into this second category.

Is Pam a workaholic? Not really. At least, not in the way we have defined that term in this book. Pam is in full control of her life; she has an identity apart from her work; and she has a diversity of interests. But looking at her track record may imply that she *has* to be a workaholic.

During high school Pam was a member of the National Honor Society and was active in the school choir and various clubs. She completed her Bachelor of Business Administration degree by age twenty-seven, all the while maintaining a full-time career as an executive with a major national corporation. She left the corporate arena at age twenty-seven to become a college professor. By age twenty-nine she was the dean of Great Lakes Community College in Michigan. By age thirty she was also a regional director of two of the college's satellite campuses.

If you ask Pam her secret of rapid success, she'll tell you, "I use over-achievement in spurts. It's not an ongoing way of life for me. I control it like a spigot. If I feel I am making steady progress in life, I am content to maintain a continuous work flow. If, however, an obstacle is put before me or I'm dealt an unexpected setback, I can open the floodgates and pour myself into a challenge. Working eighteen-hour days, including Saturdays, becomes the norm. I become indefatigable. I arrive earlier than anyone else, stay later, and produce more. Once my career has moved to a new level or a career setback has been compensated for, I'm content to resume a more normal routine again."

Pam's ability to put on and take off the cloak of excessive working has been a convenience for her. Like most conveniences, it has made life easier in some ways but it has also come at a high price. Pam has never been married and, thus, when she decides to work marathon days (or weeks), she does not have to find babysitters or worry about housekeeping or cooking meals. Conversely, during times of less stressful work she comes home to an empty apartment. (In fact, she has at times moved back with our parents for extended periods just for the fellowship factor.)

For Pam, temporary over-achievement is functional. While in undergraduate school she was in no rush. She was content to attend classes, study, and hold down a weekend job like most other college kids. After graduating and accepting an entry level position with a major corporation, however, it was time to prove her worth; so she applied for and accepted five transfers in four years. Each move offered her a new position with more responsibility and more money.

When Pam attained the highest point of middle management open to her, she then relaxed a bit for a year or so. She took time to enjoy her accumulated earnings. She bought a new car and all new furniture for her apartment. She vacationed in Tennessee, Nevada, and Arizona. She attended some night school classes and also became more involved than ever before in her church. Life was a lot of fun. Then, after an annual review in which she was told that company policy mandated that she could not apply for a senior management position until she was at least thirty years old, she explained that "her policy" was not to run in place so long. She resigned.

"After exploring several options, it occurred to me that the field of higher education had the best opportunities for women," recalls Pam. "So, I used my savings to support myself for sixteen months while I completed an MBA degree. I then researched newly developing colleges which would have executive positions opening as the campuses grew. I joined the faculty of one, but I pushed day and night for administrative responsibilities. After just one year I was chairman of the business and accounting department; eighteen months later I was named dean of arts and sciences. Now, I'm content again."

Pam is like other career women who have found that success often *requires* women to become part-time over-achievers at different times of their lives. Understanding this necessity can make it easier to cope with.

One woman who had to come to grips with on-and-off-again bouts of over-achievement was Roberta A. Grimes of Plymouth, Massachusetts. Roberta is an accountant and a lawyer, and a wife and mother of three children . . . and an over-achiever, at times. I contacted her and asked her to explain to me how she learned to find balance in her hectic life. Here is what she wrote back:

"Perhaps no woman really sees herself as she clearly is, but truly I don't consider myself a workaholic. I do what I want to do with a vengeance, but I don't enjoy working for its own sake. And when my work and my family clash, my family wins out. I think it has to be that way.

"In case it might help, I'll tell you a little of my history. I was second in my class in high school and did well at Smith College, and then floundered a bit professionally. I was an accountant, an economic consultant, and a computer programmer. I worked on the fringes of insurance and investments. In truth, I didn't know what I wanted to do with my life (other than writing, which I had forbidden myself to do; more about that in a moment).

"Eventually I married, and when I was twenty-six my husband got sick of my constantly saying I was going to go to law school someday. He prodded me to enroll. (Law school had been my father's ambition for me, as writing was my mother's. How odd it is that we so often end up living out our parents' dreams in spite of ourselves.) I had my first child during my third year of law school, and I practiced part-time briefly. But I hated it. Practicing law felt hideously dull and pointless; I wasn't really helping anyone. So, I had two more children instead, although eventually it became clear that I couldn't go on having children forever as a way of escaping the practice of law.

"In 1981 I discovered financial planning in a *Time* magazine article. And all the lights went on. Financial planning would let me use my law degree and all my prior experience, and best of all, it would save me from ever having to practice law again! I completed the two-year Certified Financial Planner program in eight months by doubling up on all the courses (which is typical of me; when I set out to do something, I do it quickly). And I opened my financial planning office in August of 1982. My children were then two, four, and five-and-a-half years old.

"Between 1982 and 1987, I worked sixty-hour weeks. My one-person office with a part-time secretary moved in the first year to a new facility four or five times larger. Within a year after that we had opened additional offices in three other towns. At its height, Freedom Financial Services, Inc., employed fourteen people and did tens of millions of dollars a year in business. Certainly I was a workaholic then: I can remember feeling torn when I left my baby to go to work on Saturday mornings, and feeling guilty about getting home later than my husband each evening. I was revved-up all the time, going at ninety miles an hour.

"My moment of truth came early in 1986 when my housekeeper was stopped for drunken driving while she was bringing my five-year-old son home from school. The police said she couldn't even walk. Of course I fired her, and I arranged things so my new housekeeper had no child care duties: my son went to an extended-day program until 5:00, and my daughters (then seven and nine) came home at 3:30 and were on their own (but with the new housekeeper on hand at all times) until 5:30.

"We limped along like that for almost a year, but it was gradually becoming clearer to me that my children needed me more. So, early in 1987, I sold my business and moved into an office attached to my home, where I could continue to do financial planning on a part-time basis and tend to my family *first* of all.

"Even though I had been (or at least had appeared to be) the consummate workaholic for more than five years and I was suddenly slowed to a crawl, this change didn't seem like a sacrifice. In fact, it felt like the best of all worlds; I didn't miss the corporate grind at all. My children's grades improved, my husband was much happier, and my life became altogether wonderful.

"One lucky break—although it didn't seem so at the time—was the fact that financial planning as a profession suffered drastically from the changes made by the Tax Reform Act of 1986. Even now I am reduced to about fifty clients, and I do the bulk of my work for just three or four major ones. That gives me lots of free time to do what my mother had wanted me to do all along, and that is become a writer.

"Writing is a form of mental possessiveness. Either you

have it or you don't have it, and if you have it you can squash it for awhile but you can't deny it forever. I wrote obsessively as a child: poems first, then stories, then novels. But I decided at sixteen that I had a choice: I could either starve in a garret as a writer, or I could give up writing and have a career and marriage and a normal life. I chose normalcy. I didn't write another word of creative writing until I was thirty.

"During most of my fourth decade, writing was someting I did instead of knitting or watching television. I didn't care about being published. I just rewrote versions of the same novel over and over (at least ten times; I've lost count), vastly enjoying it. Then in 1985, while Freedom Financial Services was still going strong, I took the significant step of attending a one-day seminar on getting published and I decided to give it a stab. I actually found a literary agent willing to take me on, but he soon dropped me when after a few tries he failed to sell the novel and two nonfiction proposals he had initially been so enthusiastic about. It was then that I decided that writing was probably a complete waste of my time and that I should never write another word.

"I kept that intention for all of 1986. It was a horrible year, and not just because of a lack of writing: we were investors in a company that failed that year and took a lot of our money with it. Early in 1987 I developed an ulcer, and while I know that the tension over the business failure may have been part of the cause, I really think not having writing as an outlet was the main problem. So, my selling my business and cutting back to motherhood in the spring of 1987 was done at least partly for health reasons.

"It was then that I started to write again. I discovered (to my amazement) that I could write other novels, too, and I did at least one draft each of three more novels over the next fifteen months. Then I attended a week-long writers' conference where I received help from superb instructors and I also found a new literary agent to start representing my work.

"My friends say that when it comes to writing I am definitely a workaholic. I do work hard at it, but that's mostly because I love it and because when I'm in the midst of something (a chapter, even a whole novel) I feel driven to reach the end as quickly as possible for fear I might somehow 'lose' it. But even when I'm in the thick of writing, my family still comes first.

"That's the thing about workaholism for women. No matter how much of a workaholic one is, the family still comes first. I'm a Christian, so I believe in being submissive to my husband, and not just for religious reasons: life simply *works* better when the man is the head of the family. I know. I've tried it both ways. And family life is food and drink for everyone, no less for the wife than for the husband and children; so, for the wife to submit is not a sacrifice. She benefits as much as anyone does. (Of course, I have a terrific husband.) Choosing a mate is one of the most important decisions in life.

"It took some time for my husband to accept my writing. Ten years, as a matter of fact. He never insisted I give it up, but he did begrudge me the time I spent on it. I used to get up at four or five o'clock while I was working full-time, just to write for a couple of hours and not have to cut into my evenings with him.

"I used to think it was possible to have everything: marriage, family, career. But now I know it really isn't possible to have everything, simply because children need heavy maternal commitment and if they don't get it they suffer grievously.

"For a woman who does put her husband and children first, in a very real sense it *does* become possible to have everything: now I have (Thank you, God!) a wonderful marriage and terrific children and plenty of time to do what I adore doing. Now, if only I could be published. . . .

"It's only fair to add that my husband is a successful physician. He has never really needed my help in supporting the family, which is one reason I've been able to cut back so severely on my financial planning and concentrate on uncompensated writing. I won't go on this way forever; if my writing never sells, eventually I'll return to more regular work. But not until my son Thomas goes off to college. And Thomas is only nine.

"Clearly, ours looks like a workaholic marriage from the outside, although it doesn't feel like one from the inside. It just feels right."

As we have seen in these profiles of Pam Hensley and Bobbi Grimes, women who lead active lives usually do not seek an ongoing "perfect balance" between work and pleasure. The balance is usually calculated by averaging the months of frantic over-achievement with the months of business as usual. This odd pace is either mandated by specific demands put on women or it is their individual choice to work this way.

THE IDEAL LIFESTYLE

A study conducted a few years ago by Market Opinion Research indicated that nearly half the women polled said the ideal lifestyle would be to stay home while the children were young, then combine homemaking with an outside job the rest of their working years. Ideal, maybe, but costly, too.

"An at-home mother [is] prey to all the nonsensical joys, gnawing doubts, culture shock, insecurities and ambiguities that so often overtake former executive women," writes Andree Aelion Brooks in *Children of Fast-Track Parents* (New York: Viking, 1989). "Neither totally domesticated nor totally committed to a lifelong career, such women become hybrid people, inhabiting—for the period of their lives they choose to stay home—a kind of no-woman's land, one foot here and one foot there, members of both camps yet totally fulfilled by neither" (p. 211).

Both Pam and Roberta found this to be true. They dealt with it in different ways: Pam avoided marriage altogether (for now, at least) and Roberta decided that submissiveness to her husband and leadership for her children were her two most important roles if she wanted to advance herself *and* be content.

No one is saying it will be easy, particularly for the woman who has known power and prestige in a career field. For her to "come home" will be agonizing at first. As Andree A. Brooks admits, "The message that comes across is clear: if you are planning to stay home, be prepared for social stigma and little social sanction to convince you that what you are doing is genuinely worthwhile; accept the fact that this is a period in history when full-time motherhood (however valuable) has been devalued by your peers; don't over-compensate; instead, sit back and relax and take time to enjoy that child" (p. 214).

If it bothers you to think that while you are home for a respite others may be getting way ahead of you, take consolation in the fact that research shows that isn't always the case. According to "Giving Workaholics the Business" in *Success*, May, 1984, a study of 1,495 MBA graduates from the University of Texas revealed that workaholics may earn slightly higher salaries than non-workaholics, but they don't always advance up the corporate ladder as quickly. Explains analyst Susan Mosier, "Workaholics often lag behind in promotions in certain fields because their single-minded devotion to work stunts their development into the sorts of well-rounded individuals often sought for high management positions."

I am convinced that women who work hard but also build in time for rest and a change of pace do, indeed, achieve more than people who just work nonstop. From a Christian viewpoint, it seems as though the necessity for "scheduled rest" is one of the primary lessons in the Bible. The Old Testament laws of agriculture called for using the land for six years and then letting it lie fallow every seventh year. The week was designed to have six workdays followed by a day of rest and meditation and worship. We all need a break now and then.

The hardworking female who forgets how to rest winds up out of control. The Bible warns that this person's "days are sorrows" and his or her "heart taketh not rest at night" (Ecclesiastes 2:23). We all know that television is filled with hundreds of commercials for aspirin, water beds, tranquilizers, alcohol, sleeping pills, books on hypnotism, vibrating pillows, and subconscious programming tapes, all designed to provide a cure for the heart that taketh not rest at night. Ironically, the only real cure for anxiety is to pull the plug on things for awhile. Ease up ... back off ... shift down. Even machines and engines need cool-down time and periodic preventive maintenance checks.

Back in chapter three we heard from successful Christian women like Mary Lou Carney and Jonellen Heckler who noted that there were clear distinctions between women who were outright workaholics and others who worked hard for a limited time (long enough to pay off the second car or to put junior and sissy through college). There is a long list of reasons why a woman may need to become a temporary over-achiever: her husband may be recovering from an illness and be too sick to support the family; a nation may be at war and need its women to work in the factories while the men are on the battle fronts; a new bride may wish to work for a few years before having children so that a car and home and furniture can be procured. These reasons and others are normal, logical, and admirable. Performing temporary hard work is not the same as workaholism.

Emotional transitions can sometimes also induce women to take on extra work, drawing them to do things that go beyond the call of normal duty. If a woman loses her husband due to death or divorce, she may begin to accept opportunities to be busy every night of the week either to avoid loneliness or to prove to others that her life is not "missing" anything. If a career woman is suddenly confronted with early or forced retirement, she may begin to sew, do crafts, initiate spring house-cleaning, or start in on any number of other activities to prove to herself she is no less productive than when she was employed.

One such case is Paula Greene, who faced "empty-nest syndrome" at age 36 when her third and youngest child left for college. Being alone all day was emotionally traumatic for Paula. There was no laundry to do; no lunches needed to be packed; no one had to be picked up after ball practice at school. Paula missed her children terribly, and the fact that she no longer had offspring-related duties to perform only served to amplify her loneliness.

Paula dealt with her problem in two extreme ways. At first, she stayed in bed almost all the time. Since there was no reason to get up, she didn't. She went to bed early, slept late in the morning, and took long afternoon naps. After nearly a month of such pouting, she began to work so much she seldom had any sleep at all. She visited friends and relatives; she played bingo three mornings each week; she joined a glee club; she signed up to be a reader to the blind at the Veterans' Hospital; and she worked at the local Salvation Army meal site. Within a second month she was on the verge of a physical breakdown.

Finally, one day a friend came to see Paula. She told her gently, but directly, that Paula was overextending herself in an effort to convince herself she had not been discarded by her children. Paula scoffed at this idea at first, but the more her friend talked, the more Paula began to face the truth. She had been a mom for so many years, she didn't know how to relax and just be herself. She had an emotional need to obtain a replacement identity for the one she had lost. Her friend empathized with the dilemma, for six years earlier she had gone through a similar problem.

"How did you learn to cope with it?" asked Paula.

"Not by working myself to death, that's for sure," said her friend. "The key is balance. You need to be involved in some sort of work, but it has to be something that puts something back into you. You can't drain your energies day after day and expect to stay healthy and happy."

"What did you do? How did you find the balance?"

Paula's friend smiled. "By going back to school," she answered. "I enrolled for two courses per semester at the local community college. The homework was a definite challenge for me—especially after having been out of high school for nearly 20 years—but I enjoyed learning new things and meeting new people. It was stimulating, rewarding . . . even fun. It took me four years, but I completed the two-year degree in social work. Now I'm a director at the state employment office. I'm as happy now as I was when I was raising my family."

Paula took her friend's advice. She found that balance was, indeed, better than over-achievement extremism. Work was a good thing, but it needed to be something that not only contributed to the benefit of others but was also of benefit to Paula.

OVERVIEW

In this chapter we have gained several insights into the kind of women who know how to make hard work their servant rather than succumbing to the reverse situation.

We noted that these women see a temporary situation of unusually taxing work requirements as something good, and that even Christian women can have a variety of justifiable reasons for choosing to work excessive hours and under greater stress for a limited time. They seem to succeed best when they know why they are working extra hard, how long it will probably endure, and what the expected result is to be.

We further noted that since females are the primary caretakers in a family (and the only one of the two sexes capable of giving birth), career women have to face some hard choices about family responsibility whenever they contemplate increasing their normal workloads. Without an understanding husband, a strong support team (baby-sitters, housekeepers), and self-sufficient children, it can be very difficult. In response to these difficulties, some women have bypassed marriage and/or child rearing or have opted to stay home until their children are grown.

Additionally, we noted that, fair or not, it is nearly impossible for a wife to earn as much or more than her husband unless she is willing to work extra hours. The frustration of this may, at times, motivate women to work so long and hard, they forget how to turn it off and relax again. They become obsessed with work, to the point of thinking of it day and night. The biblical answer to this is to plan periods of rest, rather than rely on such "crutches" as sleeping aids or alcohol.

And, finally, we discovered that many of the fears that working women have about losing ground in their career tracks if they spend time at home are overrated. In fact, these women may be helping themselves advance even faster since it is the socially complete person who more often gains a promotion than the workaholic who specializes in just one area.

During the war in Vietnam, I was a chaplain's bodyguard with the military police. The chaplain I worked for had a phrase painted across the front of our jeep: "Workin' Like the Devil for the Lord!"

One day this chaplain told me, "You know, Sarge, whenever I get assigned to a war zone like this, I work fifteen hours a day, I get shot at, I don't eat at regular intervals, and my chapel is whatever jungle clearing I may be able to stand in between battles. But it all makes me feel needed, vital, alive. When I later get rotated back to the States for a couple of years of routine duty, it seems like life is going in slow motion, as if I'm running on standby power. This is going to sound crazy to you, but I prefer it here."

At the time, it did sound a bit crazy. But now, nineteen years later, it doesn't. I understand how much better it is to be active and useful and progressive. We all need those feelings. . . . even if, at times, it calls for us to become temporary over-achievers.

EIGHT

Having It All

It's not so much how busy you are, but why you are busy.
The bee is praised. The mosquito is swatted.

—Marie O'Connor

ONE OF THE MOST DIFFICULT INTERVIEWS I have ever conducted as a writer for *The Saturday Evening Post* was with British actress Jill Ireland.

On the surface, Jill seemed to personify the woman who "had it all." When I talked with her she had been happily married for twenty years to film star Charles Bronson, was the mother of seven children, and had been blessed with the kind of career that had allowed her to work as much or as little as she chose. Unlike most moms, she was in the enviable position of being able to control her work flow. With her husband's blessing and her family's support, she had slowly stepped up her professional pace over the years and had worked more and more as her children had needed her less and less. She was one of the "lucky" ones. Truly, she "had it all."

So why did I dread calling her hotel room in Dallas on April 26, 1989, and asking her the familiar secrets-of-your-success questions that I'd asked so many times of so many famous people? Because this time, the woman who "had it all" also had terminal cancer and was in Dallas to undergo painful treatment to slow the disease's persistent, advancing pace.

What had first surfaced as a small lump under Jill's right arm had spread to her thyroid, chest wall, shoulders, and lungs. A private person, she had initially been determined to keep her sickness a secret for as long as possible. Her elderly parents in Great Britain had health problems of their own and didn't need to worry long-distance about hers, she confided to me. But one of the Hollywood gossip tabloids had heard of her frightening diagnosis and had announced to her its plans to tell the world. Did she have any comment? the tabloid reporter asked. She realized that she quickly had to "go public" in order to spare her family the pain of learning about her cancer through blaring headlines in the crass, exploitive journalism style of a gossip sheet. By the time I talked with her, nearly everyone who had ever inched through a supermarket checkout line had been subjected to the overly-dramatic, heart-wrenching stories that weekly tracked her losing battle with cancer.

Although the purpose of our telephone visit was not to focus on her illness but rather on the new book she had written, untangling the two topics was impossible. Her walk with cancer had given her the motivation to write not one but two best-sellers. Now it was nudging her to outline a third. Out of courtesy, I didn't ask the question that tugged at my mind; still, I wondered—would her debilitating health and decreasing energy level permit her to finish her latest project? As we talked, I felt certain that I knew the answer without asking. Jill Ireland's working days were nearly over.

By the time we said our good-byes that night, I was an enthusiastic fan of the tiny British actress, although I still don't recall ever having seen one of her films. In the course of our conversation—interrupted by frequent coughing spasms and punctuated by painful gasps for air—she convinced me, without trying, that she was not only a woman who had it all, but was also a woman who *had it all together*. Her physical strength may have diminished, but she was a powerhouse when it came to mental and spiritual health. And, interestingly, she owed part of her well-being to a carefully balanced, beautifully contented lifestyle that included work as a key component.

Through Jill I was able to see that while work can be an escape, a substitute, an excuse or a defense, it also can be a tool. The secret of its value is in its control. We who handle the tool must maintain control of it and never allow it to control us.

Jill was an expert in matters of control. She had always been able to keep work in its place and use it not as an end, but as a means to an end. She knew how to channel her energy *where* it was most needed and *when* it was most needed. During her children's growing-up years, she had chosen to work very little. If her stay-at-home policy had curtailed her chances of achieving major stardom, well, so be it. The only film roles she had accepted were those that allowed her to co-star with her husband. Work, in those days, had been an enabler—it had enabled the family to be together in one place at one time.

Later, in 1984, work expanded beyond the role of a tool to become an effective weapon against what Jill called the "horrible, grisly goblin that's living inside my chest." That year, when the cancer was first identified, a small wicker basket of pens, markers, pads, and other writing instruments was enlisted to boost her mental wellness just as chemotherapy and radiation were employed to treat her physical condition. She carried the basket to her daily therapy sessions and kept it by her bed for those long nights when the pain made sleep impossible. The result was *Life Wish*, a book that documented round #1 with cancer, and *Life Lines*, the sequel that told of her adopted son's addiction to drugs. Both books have comforted and counseled thousands of readers who have wrestled with similar problems.

"People say I'm great," she told me with a quiet laugh that night. "I'm not great. I don't see myself out there crusading. I'm afraid that I write for more selfish reasons."

During the two-year respite between her first brush with cancer and its recurrence, she used work to move her back into the mainstream of life and to help her shake off any temptation to feel sorry for herself. She committed the two-year pocket of time to accomplishing as much good as she could shoehorn into the months of remission that she was given. Her work ethic was healthy even when her body wasn't.

"It was as if I knew I was going to have those two 'good' years to do things," she said in retrospect. "I did everything I possibly could. I wrote, I coproduced two movies, I starred in a film, I went on the lecture circuit, and I was the American Cancer Society's crusade chairwoman. I look back and think I could have spread that over twenty years! But it was there to be done and I guess I was supposed to do it. So, I did it."

More than an occupation, work was a preoccupation when she desperately needed to be preoccupied. It served as a positive diversion. Whenever she was hospitalized for yet another series of treatments she always arrived at the admissions desk with a makeshift office in her luggage—word processor, tape recorder, and her usual supply of pads and markers—and goals to make her time count. When I caught up with her in Dallas, she candidly told me that she enjoyed talking about her writing far more than she liked discussing her illness. ("I'm a bit bored with reading in the tabloids that I'm going to die in six months," she said in her clipped British accent.)

On the night that we chatted, Jill hinted that work was beginning to fade in importance to her. Its usefulness was nearly spent, and now she was entering a period when rest was what she needed most of all. She was ready to let go of the work that had served her so well for so long. She wasn't giving up or giving in, she was merely moving on. She had no regrets about what she had or hadn't accomplished, and she refused to let herself play "what-if" games—what if she had had a little more time or had had a little less pain.

"I've gotten to the point where I appreciate simple things," she told me. "I don't want any of the big, fancy things. I just love the simplicity of life. I don't look ahead; I go for the moments."

WHAT DO YOU NEED TO HAVE IT ALL?

Tim Kimmel wrote in his book *Little House on the Freeway*, that Americans equate success with tangibles. Success is whatever we can count, look at, live in, polish, drive, wear, or play with, says Kimmel (Multnomah Press, 1987, p. 185). By that definition, Jill Ireland certainly was successful. She had all of the above. But did she "have it all"? If you asked her to tick off her "wish list"—as I asked her to do—you would find that yes, she had such a list, but no, it included none of the predictable trappings of the good life. She didn't mention anything that could be counted, looked at, lived in, polished, driven, worn, or played with.

"I want to be out in the air with the wind blowing on my face," she told me. "I love my family, my animals, my home. I want my health so I can be around for my youngest daughter. There are so many things I want to share with her about what I've learned."

Few of us can identify with Jill Ireland's lifestyle. We aren't movie stars, we aren't famous, we're probably not beautiful, and we can't work when and if we choose. Neither, I hope, do we suffer from serious illness. Still, there are similarities: We work hard, we make our time count, we maintain secret "wish lists," and most of us want to "have it all," although our criteria for what, exactly, the "all" is all about, may differ.

Women who are driven to be high-achievers occasionally

need to pause long enough to answer three questions related to the mysterious "have-it-all" status:

- What is my personal *definition* of "having it all"?
- Is it *possible* for me to have it all?
- Is it *necessary* for me to have it all?

If you were to ask these questions to a roomful of successful, highly motivated, or perfectionistic women you may very well touch off a chorus of different answers. For example, responses to the first one—What is my personal definition of "having it all"?—would probably run the gamut, depending on which individual was responding to the question and at what stage in life she happened to be. Wish lists are subject to change and are influenced by time, age, and circumstances. Not only do most women disagree on what "all" is all about, but they're likely to rethink and modify their definitions as their needs are met and their priorities are rearranged. There also seem to be different levels to "all" status, from the material (the new car, the house in the suburbs, the vacation in Hawaii) to the spiritual (peace of mind, contentment in God, spiritual serenity).

At one point early in her marriage, Jill Ireland desperately wanted to have a baby. She became pregnant, but then she miscarried. Rather than wait for a successful pregnancy, she decided to adopt a child because "having it all" meant having a family. Years later, when her adopted son developed a drug dependency that eventually claimed his life, "having it all" translated into seeing him healthy, happy, and free of his addiction. The evening that Jill and I became acquainted, most of her early wishes had become realities— she had her large family, and her son, Jason, at that point, was drug-free. Now, the obstacle to "all" status was cancer. Now, having it all meant having the simple things that most of us take for granted—the wind on her face, her daughter at her side, her pets at her feet.

If our "all" encompasses tangibles such as Tim Kimmel described—items we can count, look at, live in, polish, drive, wear, or play with—we probably can achieve it...at least for a little while. Just as quickly as we cross off the items on our wish list we'll probably fill in the blanks with new items to covet. However, if "all" means intangibles such as Jill Ireland described—good health, energy, a reprieve from death—we may be powerless in our drive to accomplish it.

As diverse as "all" status is, many high-achieving women would agree that at some level, somewhere between the tangibles and intangibles, comes the level at which we find the key components of work, marriage, and children.

I asked a sample of outstanding women if they thought it was possible to acquire this variety of "all." In other words, is it possible for a woman simultaneously to have a successful vocation or avocation, a happy marriage, and a well-balanced family life? Here, again, the verdict was mixed.

"Absolutely! Especially for *Christian* women," said Mary Lou Carney, the successful poet and teacher whom you met in chapter three. "Jesus said, 'I have come that you might have life, and have it to the full' (John 10:10). And I've always thought of him as an equal-opportunity Savior. Admittedly 'full' means different things to different people. To my mother it meant freshly waxed floors and 'good' children and packing boxes for missionaries. For me it means multi-book contracts, appearing regularly in *Guideposts*, seeing my son become the undefeated wrestling champ in his weight category (with the emphasis on *seeing*), having late-night talks with my husband, and knowing all—well, *most*—of my seventeen-year-old daughter's friends.

"It has to do with priorities and commitment," says Mary Lou. "A few years ago I got off the committee circuit. I bought an answering service to take my daytime calls. I weeded out everything that was sapping my time and creativity and I devoted myself with a singleness of purpose to two things—my family and my writing. In that order. This is why I go to soccer games and occasionally ride along with my husband to deliver a load of slag. It's also why my day often extends into the night and I turn down most church jobs. There is a pull my home office exerts on me every time I pass it—regardless of what the clock says. There is work to be done and ideas to be honed. 'Success' is, indeed, a personal thing—and each one of us carries her yardstick with which to measure herself as well as others. My criterion is not money. What keeps me grinding at the wheel is something more illusive and substantial. Corny as it may sound, I want to make a difference in the world. I want to touch people, to make them laugh and cry, to help them strive to be better, to show them how to like themselves. I want to entertain and educate. I want people to read me and be changed for the better.

"Perhaps that's why I feel such a peace about my diverse roles—because they are being orchestrated by a hand larger than my own. God does not force us to choose one of the following: A. successful career, B. happy marriage or C. well-balanced family life. Instead, he gives us one other option: D. all of the above," says Mary Lou.

While Mary Lou builds a convincing case, not all women share her belief that a balance can be struck between home and work. For them, this kind of "all" remains elusive.

"Definitely not," replied a Midwest businesswoman who asked to remain anonymous. "I believe that some area will suffer if a woman tries to balance marriage, family, and a job. A woman must choose what is most important to her at a particular time in her life. I don't for one minute believe that all women who say they *must* work really have to. They need to get their priorities straight and decide whether it is more important to 'get away' from their children, have possessions, etc., or to take the responsibility they have accepted by having children. If a woman can wait until her children are grown to pursue a full-time career—at home or away—she could then 'have it all.' If a woman does choose to work full-time while her children are still dependent on her, she can't help but be a part-time mother."

Judie, the young executive whom you met in chapter two, told me that she would like to tackle the challenge of balancing work with marriage. She has her career off to a fast start, but what about a social life that someday might lead to marriage and a family? She answered my question with one of her own. *"What* social life?" she asked ruefully.

Linda Mason, the attractive and bright seminarian who shared her story in chapter four, admits that she, too, would like to be married and have a family. She acknowledges that she might even be willing to put her career on hold and stay home for a while if she had children, but she's never been faced with having to make that decision. "I think women who are high-achievers sometimes intimidate men," she told me honestly. "I don't set out to do that, but it happens. Some men don't seem to feel comfortable with a woman who knows who she is and is confident of where she is in her life."

It's an old question that has been argued, dramatized, and even joked about for years. I remember one of the wonderful old segments of the TV sitcom, *The Dick Van Dyke Show,* in which Mary Tyler Moore's character, Laura, is given the opportunity to go back to work after years of full-time homemaking. She had been a professional dancer before she had married Rob (Dick Van Dyke) and had retired to have a family. Now Rob comes home from his job as a television comedy writer with the news that one of the TV studio dancers has become ill, and he has been authorized to offer the fill-in spot to Laura. Of course, he assumes that she isn't interested; after all, doesn't she love staying home to cook, clean, and care for Junior? Laura accepts the short-term assignment before he can get the words out of his mouth.

She proves to be amazing. Everyone at the studio marvels at her excellent condition and her speed in learning the rigorous dance routines. Rob is amazed (and more than a little disappointed) that in spite of the added workload she is still able to fix wonderful home-cooked meals and care for little Richie without showing either fatigue or regret at juggling the multiple roles. She so successfully balances home and career duties that she is asked to stay on with the dance troupe even after the ailing dancer returns. Again, this time, when Rob relays the offer he is certain of her response. After all, she seems happier now than she ever seemed during her stay-at-home years.

But once again she surprises him. "Are you sure they like my work?" she says, begging for affirmation. "Did they really say that they want me to stay? Was I really *that* good?"

"Then you'll take it," Rob assumes sheepishly.

"Of course not," replies Laura, collapsing into the living room couch. "I'm exhausted; I've never been so tired in all my life; every bone in my body aches."

"Huh?"

Laura explains that she only took the job because she wanted to prove to herself that she could still do it. She heaves a sigh of dismay as she reports the verdict—she can't.

On the surface, she had performed magnificently, had gotten rave reviews from everyone who mattered to her, and she seemingly "had it all." She had maintained the tiring regimen of a professional dancer, had kept a spotlessly clean home, had gotten up early each morning to assemble and refrigerate the evening meal, and had managed to be a loving companion to her husband and son. But the triple-duty routine had almost killed her! Now she was ready to trade leotards for apron, dance bar for breakfast bar, and resume the satisfying roles of full-time mom and home-maker. With the dilemma resolved, the theme song kicks in and the action fades out amid a flurry of hugs and a burst of recorded laughter.

No wonder *The Dick Van Dyke Show* was so popular. Like most successful comedy, it contained just enough truth to enable viewers to identify with it. But, to boost the laughter, everything was slightly exaggerated. Laura tried *too* hard to juggle jobs; she succeeded *too* well in her determination to be all things to all people; the dance troupe leader was *too* pleased with her performance; Rob sulked *too* much about his wife's booming career; son Richie was *too* cute; and the plot was *too* obvious. Life isn't quite like that, as we know; but when a sitcom only has thirty minutes to tell a complicated story (less, when you subtract numerous commercial breaks), who has time to be subtle?

A QUALIFIED "MAYBE"

By now it's probably obvious that it's easier to ask certain questions than to answer them. Let's go back to those three that I suggested that every high-achieving woman should put to herself.

- What is my personal definition of "having it all"?
- Is it possible for me to have it all?
- Is it necessary for me to have it all?

We've seen that the first two questions draw conflicting responses. When trying to define what "having it all" is all about, we really need to compose several lists, each involving a different level of "all." There's the material level (the "things" that Tim Kimmel mentioned); the situational level (the challenging job and happy home that concerned Mary Tyler Moore's television character); the physical level (the elusive good health and long life that Jill Ireland fought for); and the spiritual level (the serenity, peace, and contentment that we all aspire to).

After we've made our several lists, we can wrestle with

the second question: Is it possible to have it all—whatever the "all" might be? Depending on which list we're dealing with, the answer could be yes, could be no, or could be a qualified maybe. "Things" are easily attained; but situations are more difficult. With a little planning and careful budgeting, most of us can, over time, collect the material comforts and "toys" that we want. But a challenging job, a loving marriage relationship, and a harmonious family? The woman who successfully juggles those three roles—as we've seen—has to have great concentration, excellent balance, super timing, and an abundance of skills to perform well in what could be a busy three-ring circus. If truly human, she might even drop one of the "balls" from time to time.

It gets harder. The physical level of "all" status offers a new set of obstacles. As we witnessed with Jill Ireland, this level is even tougher to achieve, and sometimes clearly is out of our hands.

But if "having it all" appears to become more difficult (even impossible) as we move farther away from the simple material "things," the good news is that the highest level—the spiritual level—is the easiest of the lot to attain. It's there for our asking.

When the Apostle Paul wrote his letter to the Philippians to thank them for their support of his missionary work, he was old, tired, and imprisoned. He had endured thirty years of being mobbed, stoned, and beaten. No one would have blamed him for feeling bitter and resentful. Did he have it all? By some standards he had nothing. Yet in his letter he told his faithful Christian friends that he had never been happier. By *his* standards, he had it all.

I have learned how to get along happily whether I have much or little. I know how to live on almost nothing or with everything. I have learned the secret of contentment in every situation, whether it be a full stomach or hunger, plenty or want; for I can do everything God asks me to with the help of Christ who gives me the strength and power. (Philippians 4:11-13, *The Living Bible*)

Paul had worked out his personal definition of what "all" was all about, and he was living proof that it was attainable. He had learned to manage without material goods, even without food, and he had gotten to the place where everything he required was provided by Christ. "All" for Paul had a higher meaning—it was contentment in God. Yes, it was necessary, and yes, it was his.

PUTTING IT ALL TOGETHER

Helen Hosier is one of those warm, comfortable women who fits in anywhere. Because she is such a high-achiever, I never doubted that she belonged in this book; my only dilemma was where to put her. She would comfortably fit into any discussion of a hard-working, well-balanced, Christian wife, mother, and grandmother of *thirteen* grandchildren. In fact, if someone were to ask me to describe her in twenty-five words or less, I'd probably say, "Helen Hosier? Now, there's a woman who has it all together." In view of that, perhaps she best belongs in this chapter as an example of a woman who has it all, as well as one who has it all together.

If her name sounds familiar, let me prod your memory. She is the author of *fifty-three* books—not all under her byline—that have inspired Christians since her first one was published in 1966. While that's high-achievement, it's not why she's a likely candidate to be profiled in a book about work-prone women. In spite of her success, Helen has never been motivated by applause. Her motivation, like Paul's, comes from a desire to serve God. Her strength comes from Jesus Christ.

"My father died five months before I was born," she told me. "I remember once when I was about four years old, I was sitting on the lap of my girlfriend's father when suddenly my friend became jealous. 'This is *my* daddy, not yours,' she said. I ran to my mother and asked, 'Where's *my* daddy?' She reminded me that my father was in heaven with my heavenly Father. That experience totally colored my life. I became a very God-conscious little girl; since then the supremely motivating force in my life has been to please God."

She can't remember a time when she didn't work. She took her cue from her mother, a seamstress, who worked hard and managed to support her three children without having to leave the home. Little Helen, the youngest, would sit at her mother's feet and would memorize verses from the Bible as her mother worked on her various sewing projects. Helen came to know Scripture so well that throughout her life whenever faced with a decision or a question or a problem, she could recall a verse that was perfectly applicable. Just as any child looks to her father for guidance, she depended on her heavenly Father and found all the advice she needed.

"Even today, when I have to make a decision I always pause and say, 'God, what am I supposed to do now? How am I supposed to respond to this?' " she explained. "Psalm 32:8 says, 'I will instruct you (says the Lord) and guide you along the best pathway for your life; I will advise you and watch your progress.' It only takes a minute to ask for his instruction, and on the few occasions when I haven't done this, I've made my biggest mistakes."

She credits God with pointing her in some interesting directions, and says he has been responsible for any success she has known. For instance, when she was a young wife and mother she felt him nudge her toward starting a Christian bookstore. She had been active in a Bible study group, and the leader often had quoted books that none of the group members had heard of. When Helen tried to find the references, she learned there was no store in her hometown that carried Christian material.

"I was working as a church secretary at the time and had a little money tucked away, so I started buying books from wholesale catalogs," she said. "This was back in the days when we took our babies for walks in old-fashioned baby strollers with metal baskets in the back. I loaded our stroller with as many cards and books as I could handle, and I went door to door. I'd give my testimony and tell people how important it was for them to read good Christian literature and to raise their children on Bible study books."

The bookstore on wheels gave way to a storefront on Main Street and eventually developed into a small chain. In order to keep the shelves well stocked, she attended booksellers' conventions where she became acquainted with which books were *and weren't* available. She had definite ideas about the reading needs that weren't being fulfilled. When a publisher approached her with the suggestion that she should try her hand at the typewriter, at first she hesitated, then she asked God, then she reached for the keyboard.

"By that time I had four children," she recalled. "The first book came out in 1966, and I've had two or three published every year since then." In addition, she's never stopped working outside her home.

Helen manages her time well, has learned the art of saying "no" to an overload of obligations, and is stingy with the moments she gives to out-of-the-home activities. She loves her work, but she loves her family more. Above all, she loves her God.

The reason that Helen is my favorite example of a woman who has it all is because her "all" begins and ends with her solid relationship with her heavenly Father. After that, her other priorities fall into place in a logical order. But none takes precedent over her God. She depends upon him as much today as she did when she was a little girl growing up in Iowa as the youngest child in a single-parent home. Her day begins and ends with prayer, and every decision made in between is based on the direction he gives to her.

"I'm a goal-setter," she's admitted to me on many occasions. "At the beginning of each week I like to sit at my desk and strategize. I say to myself, *This is a new week, what are you going to do with it?*"

Then she closes her eyes and waits for God to provide the answer.

NINE

How to Unstructure Your Life

We feel guilty over pleasure so we take care not to get too much of it.
                              —Warren Oates
                              Confessions of a Workaholic

WHEN HURRICANE HUGO STRUCK THE CAROLINAS IN SEPTEMBER, 1989, one clever man saved his beautiful yacht by doing something that seemed "crazy" to his neighbors. As the strong winds and heavy waves began to push the yachts anchored off-shore toward the docks, beaches, and rock-lines, this man went out to his yacht on a small speedboat. He removed everything of personal value, then took an ax and cut a hole in the bottom of the yacht. The yacht sank into fifteen feet of water, where it waited out the hurricane.

After the hurricane was over, the man hired a tugboat to raise his yacht from below the water and to bring it to a dock. The man let it dry off and then he repaired the hole in the bottom. His total expense was $475 and he was back on the sea in one week. His neighbors found their yachts crushed and splintered all over the coastline. They had to pay $3000 deductible charges to their insurance companies and then wait four months before they could obtain replacement crafts.

There's a lesson in that little story. Sometimes we have to take some radical actions up front in order to secure greater blessings later on.

If you feel that the "hurricane" of workaholism is threatening to dash you against life's shoreline, you may need to scuttle some of your plans in order to save the ship, *i.e.*, yourself. No one can expect you to do a one-hundred-eighty-degree about-face in your life. Nevertheless, you can start today to ease away from your excessive workload.

Joanne Markle became so exhausted by doing work that "just *had* to get done," she discovered she couldn't get out of bed one morning. She had not had a heart attack, nor a nervous breakdown. She was simply too exhausted to move.

"My husband made breakfast for our three kids and drove them to school that morning," recalls Joanne, "and then he came back and sat on the side of my bed. He had been warning me for months to slow down, to remember to eat nutritious foods, to get more sleep. Instead, I had relied on coffee and candy bars, catnaps and cold showers to keep me going. Finally, it caught up to me.

"Allen knew I was not the type who could just take three months off to rest and recover. I would go nuts. So, as he sat there, he made a list of people he and I could call to tell that I would be resigning from committees and bowling teams and social organizations. Just doing that put an extra twenty hours per week into my schedule. Small sacrifices early on made it possible for me to recuperate my strength so that I didn't experience a total collapse which would have caused me to lose my job as a newspaper reporter, and my family life."

Joanne's primary mistake had been not establishing

priorities and remaining loyal to them. If she would have concentrated on her family, her church, and her job, she might never have agreed to so many other duties.

Joanne admits that there were personal matters that led to her situation of going "out of control." She had several mistaken beliefs, such as a feeling that she had to be all things to all people. It wasn't *enough* to be a good citizen, she had to be active on committees to clean up the atmosphere and to secure new books for the local library. It wasn't *enough* to be a good neighbor, she had to bowl in the morning women's league, collect dues for the neighborhood association, and arrange the summer block party. It wasn't *enough* to be a good mom, she had to be treasurer of the PTA, leader of the Girl Scout troop, and a room mother for the fourth grade.

When asked why she was driven like this, Joanne had two specific answers. First, she said, it was because she lacked personal self-esteem and second, because no one had ever taught her how to manage her time wisely or how to establish her priorities.

Joanne's self-esteem problems were caused by her shortness ("I was always the smallest kid in the class"), her embarrassment about a habit she couldn't break ("I was a chain smoker despite the fact it was a habit I deplored"), and the shame of an event that occurred in her early life ("I dated a boy my parents told me to stay away from and he took advantage of me sexually"). After seeking counseling from her minister and entering a hospital to break her nicotine dependency, Joanne had a feeling of new worth about herself. Once her emotional problems had been dealt with, she then was ready for some practical assistance in the management of her time. Let me share some tips here with you that I shared with her.

Have you ever taken five minutes to sit down and really prioritize your obligations in life? If not, you can use the

"Ranking Your Priorities" chart in this chapter to help you focus on what should matter to you. In addition, answer the questions in the quiz called "Separating Psychic Income From Stress." The answers you provide—and do be honest—will help you decide whether or not you may one day reach total exhaustion (or worse) the way Joanne Markle did.

TIME PRIORITIES

Sometimes one of the best ways to unstructure your life is to learn how to make better use of the few hours you have to work with. Whole books have been written on how to manage time effectively. You might profit from reading some of these books. For now, however, I can provide an alphabet of time management tips to help you seem to add hours to your day.

HENSLEY'S TIME MANAGEMENT ALPHABET

A. Instead of punishing yourself for wasting time, give yourself rewards when you manage time wisely. Reinforce in a positive way.

B. Dump your feelings of guilt. You cannot be all things to all people, nor can you live up to ridiculous expectations others set for you. To sit and brood over real or imagined shortcomings is a genuine waste of your time.

C. When it comes to preparing your Sunday school lesson, writing a speech, or other tasks calling for concentration, protect your privacy. Do away with the open door policy at home or at work.

D. Avoid meetings whenever possible. If you must convene a meeting for some reason, prepare a specific agenda ahead of time. And stick to it.

E. Game-plan your twenty-four-hour segments by filling out a daily schedule and planner every night before going to bed.

Stick to your game plan every day. As you complete each job, cross it off as a psychic reward.

F. Set goals. Write them down. Strive to reach them by specific dates.

G. Don't be afraid to nag if someone else's work is delaying one of your projects. The noisy wheel really does get the oil.

H. Stay healthy. Take vitamins, get regular exercise, eat nutritious foods, control your weight, and get regular medical checkups. Time spent in sickbeds is wasted time.

I. Return calls just before noon or just before 5 P.M. each day. This will prevent the other person from rambling.

J. Use commuting time to listen to cassette tapes that can teach you a new language, show you how to make public speeches, motivate you, or discuss innovative business techniques.

K. Link errands together. Instead of four trips a day, make a list, plan your route, and stop at the dry cleaners, library, bank, and grocery store in succession.

L. Instead of long coffee breaks, take five-minute *work pauses*. This will refresh you but not give you time to lose your work inertia.

M. Learn from mistakes. Don't repeat them.

N. Anticipate change, prepare for it, and adapt quickly when it comes.

O. If you can afford them, use machines that save time: self-dialing phones, hand-held miniature tape recorders, word processors, calculators, microwave ovens, dish-washers, self-defrosting refrigerators, etc.

P. Learn to make a decision: to lead, follow, or get out of the way.

Q. Eat light lunches. Heavy midday meals make you sluggish in the afternoon.

R. Have a time each day for your devotions. Draw strength from the Scriptures. Turn your burdens over to God through prayer.

S. If you work in an office at home or at work, arrange all furniture and equipment so you can reach items with minimum effort. Without having to stand, you should be able to reach wastebasket, in-out trays, typewriter or computer keyboard, intercom, and bulletin board.

T. When you are home and need to concentrate, use "override noise" (the hum of a dehumidifier, an FM radio played low) to subdue external distracting noises.

U. Carry two books with you at all times: one to read when you are caught with time on your hands and one with blank pages so you can write down any good ideas that you may develop.

V. Remember Parkinson's Law: *Work expands to fill the time available for its completion.* As such, set deadlines that are challenging and realistic.

W. Plan your work. Work your plan.

X. Never consider defeat. Concentrate on your strengths, not weaknesses.

Y. Combine tasks whenever possible. Stuff envelopes while you are talking on the phone.

Z. Build some slack time into your daily schedule (one open appointment time, a shorter lunch hour) so that unforeseen interruptions do not cause a panic.

RANKING YOUR PRIORITIES

Rank your *personal goals* according to their priorities:

___ More business challenges

___ More personal recognition

___ More education

___ More professional prestige

___ More leisure time

___ Better social standing

___ More money

___ More overall accomplishments

___ More service to God

___ More service to other people

Rank your *business goals* according to their priorities:

___ Greater productivity

___ Increased visibility

___ Higher profits

___ Stronger ethics and standards

___ Better reputation

___ Stricter product evaluations

___ Unrivaled services

___ More scientific emphasis

___ Improved customer relations

___ Superior systems analysis

___ Nicer work environment

___ Better time management

___ Continual expansion

___ More financial reserves

Rank your *personal strengths* related to church, family, and business:

___ Public speaking

___ Sense of humor

___ Math and bookkeeping

___ Personal reputation

___ Handling customers

___ Company loyalty

___ Selling by telephone

___ Product knowledge

___ Personal appearance

___ Competitive spirit

___ Years of experience

___ Talent for writing

___ Formal education

___ Ability to organize

___ Business connections

___ Time management skills

___ Never ceasing drive

___ Understanding of technology

___ Capacity for careful listening

___ Political clout

___ Ability to teach

___ Continuous spiritual growth

SEPARATING PSYCHIC INCOME FROM STRESS

If you have any doubts as to whether your long hours are motivated by enjoyment or by pressure, use this quick true-or-false test as a guide. If you are motivated by enjoyment, the majority of your answers will be "true."

___ **1.** I don't rely on stimulants or pills to keep me going.

___ **2.** I don't seem exhausted even though I only sleep four to seven hours per night.

___ **3.** I seldom suffer from headaches or backaches.

___ **4.** I pace myself well and use good time management practices.

___ **5.** I like and appreciate my colleagues, clients, and prospects.

___ **6.** I am not afraid to delegate certain jobs.

___ **7.** I am not threatened by reasonable quotas, deadlines, or goals.

___ **8.** When out at social events, I do not hide what I do for a living.

___ **9.** I understand and respect the need for daily exercise.

___ **10.** Losing a sale is a disappointment, but not a cause for a day of depression.

TIME FOR TWENTY QUESTIONS
(How Do You Rate?)

Yes No   Do you:

___ ___   **1.** Start the day before thinking through what has to be done?

___ ___   **2.** Start a job before thinking it through?

___ ___   **3.** Leave jobs before they are completed?

___ ___   **4.** Do the easy or less important work first before the more important (and possibly more unattractive) work?

___ ___   **5.** Assign tasks without specifying quantity, quality, and time?

___ ___   **6.** Assign difficult tasks without checking to see if your employee needs help?

___ ___   **7.** Have trouble saying no even though you can't see when a task will get completed?

___ ___   **8.** Do most of the work rather than assigning someone to help you?

___ ___   **9.** Do work by hand that a machine could do?

___ ___   **10.** Do things that aren't really your job?

___ ___   **11.** Spend a lot of time doing the things you have always done and are good at doing?

Yes No Do you:

— — **12.** Feel the best way to do things is the way you have always done them?

— — **13.** Start projects that you have little interest in or know you probably won't finish?

— — **14.** Make sure the short, easy tasks get done early?

— — **15.** Often operate by crisis management?

— — **16.** Handle a large number of different jobs?

— — **17.** Handle concerns of employees immediately when requested?

— — **18.** Socialize daily during business hours either in person or via telephone with friends?

— — **19.** Get distracted, while working, by such things as newspapers, friends who drop in, low-priority mail, etc.?

— — **20.** Make several trips outside your office rather than grouping errands together for one trip?

To rate yourself, count the number of *yes* answers and the number of *no* answers. If you answered *yes* more than *no* you have a lot of work ahead. If you have five to ten *yes's*, you can improve the effective use of your time. If you answered *yes* to more than fifteen questions, you may be in trouble.

DAILY SCHEDULE AND PLANNER

Today's Date: _____

This Week's Goal: _____

This Month's Project: _____

My Life Priorities	Today's Errands	Typing, Sewing, and Other Family Duties
	Ongoing Projects	

Letters to Write	Phone Calls to Make	Appointments and Scheduled Interviews	Miscellaneous

SUGGESTED READINGS ON TIME MANAGEMENT

Bliss, Edwin C. *Getting Things Done.* New York: Bantam Books, 1980, 196 pages.

Doyle, Michael and David Straus. *How to Make Meetings Work.* New York: Wyden Books, 1976, 298 pages.

Engstrom, Ted W. and Alex R. MacKenzie. *Managing Your Time: Practical Guidelines on the Effective Use of Time.* Grand Rapids, Michigan: Zondervan Publishing House, 1967, 207 pages.

Harvey, Karen. *Managing Time, Managing Life: The NOW System.* New York: NAL Books, 1986, 224 pages.

Hensley, Dennis E. *How to Manage Your Time.* Anderson, Indiana: Warner Press, 1989, 86 pages.

Jones, Curtis H. "The Money Value of Time," *Harvard Business Review.* July-August 1968, pp. 94-101.

Lakein, Alan. *How to Get Control of Your Time and Your Life.* New York: Peter E. Wyden Publishers, Inc., 1973, 203 pages.

Lobingier, John L., Jr: *Business Meetings That Make Business.* Toronto: Collier-MacMillan Limited, 1969, 146 pages.

Machlowicz, Marilyn. *Workaholics.* New York: Mentor Executive Library, 1980, 198 pages.

MacKenzie, R. Alex. *The Time Trap.* AMACOW, New York, 1972.

Parkinson, C. Northcote. *Parkinson's Law.* Boston: Houghton-Mifflin, 1957, 113 pages.

Scott, Dru. *How to Put More Time in Your Life.* New York: Signet Books, 1980, 226 pages.

Still, Henry. *Of Time, Tides, and Inner Clocks.* Harrisburg, Pennsylvania: Stackpole Books, 1972.

Terry, George R. *Supervision.* Homewood, Illinois: Richard D. Irvin, Inc., 1978.

Webber, Ross A. *Time and Management.* New York: Van Nostrand Reinhold Co., 1972.

CONFRONTING BURNOUT

Although the alphabet listing of time management tips we have just reviewed will help you become better organized and better able to cope with life's daily challenges, you will still need to convince yourself that cutting back on overall activities is mandatory. No matter how well you manage your time, the fact remains: there are still only twenty-four hours in a day. When you try to do thirty hours of work in twenty-four hours of time, the same thing happens to you that happens to an engine that never cools down—you burn out. Everyone needs to slow down from time to time. Even you.

We live in a fast world these days. People used to wait three days for a stagecoach. Today, they get upset if they miss one section of a revolving door.

Speed seems to be the primary concern of everyone. Fast-food restaurants, one-hour dry cleaners, high-speed computers, automatic-developing cameras, and supersonic transports are routine parts of our whirlwind way of life. Is it any wonder, then, that from time to time we "overload" our mental and physical circuits and cause burnouts?

Burnout can sometimes become so advanced it can manifest physical symptoms, such as insomnia, headaches, backaches, weight loss, nervousness, and exhaustion. It can also reveal itself in behavioral patterns. For example, if you increase your rate of absenteeism at church or work, if you overreact to criticism, or if you make snap decisions about people, you may be suffering from burnout. If left unchecked, this condition has been known to lead to marital problems, alcoholism, or drug abuse.

To be a successful and happy person, you need to have enthusiasm, optimism, individualism, and imagination. Being only human, however, you will sometimes find it difficult to maintain a good and constant grip on these four factors. Life is not always manageable. Quite often, you are made to take the bitter with the sweet.

Fortunately, if you are wise enough to recognize burnout for what it is, you can also be wise enough to overcome it. Let me offer you ten ways to reverse the feeling of being burned out.

The first two things you need to do are get adequate sleep and get adequate exercise. The body *requires* rest. The requirements vary from person to person, but a minimum of six hours per night is recommended. Going to bed a little earlier than usual on occasion, taking a catnap after supper, and enjoying a long nap on Sunday afternoons will give new vitality to your system. Similarly, a brisk half-hour walk at lunchtime and an evening or two of bowling or racquet-ball will add stamina to your physical make-up. If you allow your body to deteriorate, your stress circuits will overload much quicker.

The next two things you need to do are to make positive uses of your past and future. You should keep a diary or journal of your greatest days and key accomplishments. Read this record frequently and draw encouragement from your past successes. Similarly, get into the habit of always planning something to look forward to and be excited about. Call a close friend and set up a lunch date for next week; arrange a weekend of camping for early next month; sign up to attend a Bible conference in Florida next winter. Plan always to have a future-event "carrot" dangling in front of you.

The fifth tip is to study something new. Mental stimulation is a cure-all for both depression and fatigue. Choose a foreign language you would like to become conversant in and get training tapes from the public library to practice with; or choose a section of the world you'd like to know more about—the Middle East, China, South Africa—and read books about its history and magazine articles about its current events; or sign up for a class in art appreciation and spend time in museums expanding your cultural awareness;

or select a book of the Old Testament and do a chapter-by-chapter analysis of it; or have fun learning to strum a guitar. By giving yourself an enjoyable challenge and by opening new avenues of learning to yourself, you will add zest and spark to your life.

The sixth suggestion is for you to learn to say "No." You simply cannot be all things to all people. If you accept more responsibilities than you have time to handle properly, you will generate incredible amounts of worry, frustration, and stress. When you are approached to handle something and you do not have the time to do it, be honest and direct enough to say no. It may be hard at first, but if you constantly remind yourself that it is for your own good, as well as the good of the project you are being drafted to help, you will soon be able to reject offers without feeling guilty.

A seventh tip is for you to travel more. Burnout can sometimes be caused by boredom which is compounded by a lack of diversity in surroundings. If you have been living in the same home or working in the same building for five years, plan a change-of-place. Get out and see new faces, travel new roads, eat at different restaurants, jog in someone else's neighborhood, attend a concert in a nearby town, vacation somewhere besides "the lake" this summer, shop in a different mall, walk through a different branch of the public library. Keep in mind that even in regard to locales, variety is the spice of life.

An eighth idea is for you to develop a hobby. John F. Kennedy used to unwind by reading mystery novels. Winston Churchill found serenity in painting landscapes. Anyone whose life is active (and surely yours is, or else you wouldn't be reading this book) needs to find an avenue of escape from the "regular grind." Choose a hobby, such as stamp or coin collecting, gardening or woodworking, which will so totally occupy your concentration, you will be able to put your other worries in the background for an hour or two. Just as traveling to different locations can be mentally stimulating, so, too, can working on different projects.

A ninth suggestion is for you to set realistic and flexible goals for yourself. Goal-setting is a great idea for anyone; however, if your goals are not attainable or your time frame is unreasonably demanding, you will burn yourself out trying to reach the unreachable. Be a little more compassionate with yourself. Set goals which are challenging, but don't try to reorganize your life, your career, or the world in ten days. You don't need that kind of anxiety or frustration.

The final tip is for you to set up a support group of friends and peers who can offer you advice and encouragement. Do this by inviting people with common interests and objectives to a weekly or monthly talk session. Keep the meeting's tone informal, but have a procedure to follow each time. One meeting can be a social hour and idea exchange session; another meeting can feature a guest speaker who will help the group to overcome a common problem (time management, household budgeting, child rearing, beauty aids, marital relations, spiritual growth). Just knowing you're not "in this alone" can often be the greatest form of encouragement you'll ever need.

These ten tips are by far not the only procedures for confronting and coping with burnout, but they will get you on the right path. Naturally, if you are experiencing severe physical disorders, it is always wise to consult with your family physician.

Sometimes the most important aspect of restructuring your life from the depressing, oppressive, and tedious to the joyful, exciting, and energetic is to concentrate more on the regeneration of the soul than the mind or body. Let's look next at that aspect.

THE SOUL OF THE MATTER

Have you ever wondered why some missionaries, ministers, and other servants of God can seem to work endlessly without showing signs of exhaustion, yet other people seem ready to collapse after putting in a standard eight-hour work day? Part of the secret is attitude.

The Bible tells us, "Whatever you do, in word or deed, do everything in the name of the Lord Jesus" (Colossians 3:17). People who begin a task with the attitude that they are doing their work as to the Lord find that they not only do better work, but also enjoy it more. What if you cleaned house in the name of the Lord? . . . or cooked meals in the name of the Lord? . . . or washed clothes and cared for your children and planned your budget and planted your roses and did your mending and visited the infirm and sang a church special in the name of the Lord? Wouldn't that lift your spirits and enhance your ability? You know it would!

All work done well and to the glory of God is pleasing in his eyes, and should also be in ours. Theologian and orator William Tyndale once wrote, "Indeed, there is a difference between washing dishes and preaching the Word of God; *but,* as touching to please God, there's no difference at all." I agree with this. So, if you have put undo stress on yourself about the "value" of your work, it is more a problem of your attitude than your work performance.

SUMMARY

In this chapter we saw that excessive workers seldom can withdraw "cold turkey" from their heavy workloads. They can, however, take steps in the right directions by establishing priorities and then withdrawing from superfluous obligations which do not relate to the priorities.

We also noted that putting some time management tips into practice can create better personal organization and, thus, seem to add hours to a person's day. This "new time" can reduce stress and tension.

Additionally, we discovered how to recognize conditions

of burnout and how to cope with it, as well as how to change our attitude about our work by doing all that we do to the glory of God.

So, if you've been on the merry-go-round too long, follow the advice in this chapter and learn how to sit out some of the whirling.

Epilogue: Work in Progress

Talk about timing.

Midway through this book project, my wife Rose decided to go back to work. It wasn't an all-of-a-sudden kind of decision; we had talked about it since Jeanette, our youngest, had started fifth grade. Still, it seemed ironic. Suddenly I was living most of the issues I was discussing in the book. The man with all the answers was finally having to cope with all the questions. And what did this experience teach me? Let me put it this way: I've learned a lot since I've known it all.

My wife and I were latecomers to the two-income family situation. Rose holds B.A. and M.A. degrees in elementary education and she had taught school for the first couple of years of our marriage. Once we started our family, however, Rose wanted to be a full-time mom. It was her decision, and I supported her in it. So, for the next twelve years we became a one-income family. With two youngsters, a busy husband, and personal responsibilities which ranged from teaching Sunday school to assisting at the public library, Rose never lacked for plenty to do.

However, once our children were old enough to relieve Rose and me of much of their care, Rose began to talk about entering the work force again. I told her that she didn't need to do this since my career had evolved to a point where we were financially comfortable. I had missed the real issue, however, which was that Rose had skills and talents she enjoyed maximizing. She *wanted* to work. It would add an element of self-esteem, personal fulfillment, and challenge to her life.

At this point let me explain that Rose is a perfectionist but not a workaholic; I'm a workaholic but not a perfectionist. Her way is better. We both achieve a lot, but for different reasons. She'll attack a job with great intensity and not stop until it's completed exactly right. Once she's finished, she feels satisfied with her performance and needs no applause from any audience. She knows that she has performed well and that she has earned her "time off."

Me? I attack a job with the same enthusiasm, but instead of concentrating on results, I focus on activities. To Rose, work is a means to an end; to me, it's an end in itself. Hers is a much healthier attitude, and she's helping me to change mine.

I had mixed feelings when Rose landed a job as an office coordinator the very first day she went out for an interview. I couldn't help but be proud of how readily "employable" she was; however, I also couldn't help but think about how her new job might cause changes in my life, *i.e.*, my well-established routine. If that sounds selfish, you're right, but give me credit for gut-level honesty.

Rose loved her new job and being back "in the public." She quickly became a Jill-of-all-trades at the small magazine publishing house where she worked. She ran the computers, worked the switchboard, attended staff meetings, proofread the galleys, handled the business correspondence, and set up appointments. After just two months on the job she was given a raise and the company put a metal name plate on her door signifying "you're one of us."

Whereas this was all very fulfilling for my wife, it proved to be a nightmare for me. Rose had to commute forty-five minutes to and from work. That meant she was gone from 7:00 A.M.-6:00 P.M. most days. Her schedule was absolutely inflexible. (She was even docked half a day's pay when she took off three hours to attend a funeral one afternoon.)

We had always operated on a fifty-fifty basis, but now I assumed all of Rose's duties that had to be executed in that eleven-hour period. I had to run Nathan to the doctor's office for allergy shots every Monday afternoon in addition to driving Jeanette to the orthodontist and to her piano lessons and to the library. I was the one who showed up solo at parent-teacher conferences and served as a chaperone for school field trips and had to be available when the TV repairman came to our house and take the cars (now two) in for lube work or a tune-up.

I was quick to voice my frustrations, but also quick to try to make things work out best for all. We initiated an increase in weekly allowance payments for the kids, accompanied by a new list of extra household chores they needed to assume. Rose and I both cut back on our social plans in order to have more evenings at home to keep up with bill paying, laundry, ironing, grass cutting, yard work, and house cleaning.

All of this helped, but did not solve the problem. Schedule conflicts continued to arise. Before Rose took on her new job, she and the kids used to travel with me on weekends. Now, with Rose working late each Friday night, I traveled without the family. The kids hated that. Mom's job was knocking them out of Saturday morning room service, hotel swimming pools, airplane trips, and the fun of seeing new cities. They were not subtle in sharing their disappointment with Rose. But to their surprise, Mom said she missed the weekend trips, too.

As summer drew nearer, the kids began to get really excited. Each year I have always accepted week-long invitations to speak at writers' conferences around the country. The family almost always goes with me. I arrange things so that I can lecture all morning and then have the afternoons free to go sightseeing with the family. The coming summer was shaping up to be one of the best times ever, with trips to Chicago, Philadelphia, Washington, D.C., a resort area in northern Michigan, and a posh hotel complex in Grand Rapids. As we talked of all we planned to do and see—Valley Forge, the Lincoln Memorial, the Smithsonian Institute—it began to dawn on us that Mom would not be coming along. She would have to stay in Indiana and go to her job.

Rose was on the horns of a dilemma. She loved her job, and she loved her family. She did not want to disappoint her employer, but she also didn't want to miss out on sharing family experiences with her children before they grew up.

Additional problems weighed on her. If I left for a three-day business trip during the summer, could she just go off to work and leave the children to fend for themselves?

After a great deal of prayer, careful thought, and family discussion, Rose settled on a compromise. She decided that, yes, it was right for her to have an outside job again; but, no, the job she had taken was not the right one for her needs nor the needs of her family. As such, she met with her employer and explained the circumstances. She agreed to work another six weeks and to train her replacement. Everyone hated to see her go, but they respected her decision. Rose then applied for a job as a teacher and went back on a nine-month schedule that coincided with our kids' schedules.

Now, lest you think this made things end "happily ever after," think again. I called this epilogue "Work in Progress" because each day Rose and I are having to learn new ways to coordinate our schedules and balance our lives. I don't have all the answers . . . but I'm learning.

If nothing else, we've learned to bend. Rose will spend all day on Saturday working on bulletin boards in her classroom. She'll stay after school on Friday nights until 9 P.M. working on the next week's lesson plans or grading papers. Naturally, I'd rather have her at home, but I've learned to appreciate her diligence. Rose is good about tolerating my work extravagances, too. When I have to lock myself in my office on holidays in order to complete a writing project, she grits her teeth but endures it.

Since parents teach more by example than by lecture, Rose and I have been sensitive to the sort of role modeling we are presenting to our two children. Many of those aspects have been quite pleasing. My son has seen me make beds, clear the table, wash the dishes, and run the vacuum cleaner so often that he has no stigma about doing such chores. To him, it's all "family work," so he pitches right in with whatever he is asked to do around the house. Similarly, my daughter is not embarrassed at school to volunteer her dad to be a "room mother" for her class. (I did ask for the creation of a new title, *i.e.*, room *father*. No one objected.)

In writing this book, Holly Miller and I did not present ourselves as experts on the subject of over-achievement and workaholism. Instead, we were, and are, searchers. We sought insights and ideas and experiences from people in all walks of life who *had previously* or *were currently* confronting work and career-related problems. This book is a compilation of the responses we received to our questionnaires, the wisdom we drew from other researchers and authors who have explored this field, the statutes and lessons found in the Bible that relate to work, and our personal feelings and views on the matters we chose to focus on in our chapters.

In closing, I would share these truths with you:

For work performance, recall Colossians 3:23, "Whatever your task, work heartily, as serving the Lord and not men."

For work reward, recall Luke 10:7, "The laborer deserves his wages."

For work self-respect, recall Ecclesiastes 5:12, "Sweet is the sleep of a laborer."

For work motivation, recall 2 Thessalonians 3:10, "If anyone will not work, let him not eat."

Keep *working* on those four standards and you'll do just fine.